MAKING MONEY

MAKING MONEY

Henry Hills

SEGUE

Cover design: Freda Mekul

publication made possible in part by a grant from
The New York State Council on the Arts

published by
THE SEGUE FOUNDATION
300 Bowery
New York, N.Y. 10012

Library of Congress Catalog Card Number 86-061581

ISBN 0–937804–25–8

INTRODUCTION

Making money has become the principal obsession & dominant focus of the decade. Where are the utopian theories, mad manifestos pressing idealistic plans, burning ideas for revolutionary improvement? If art is optimism, to whatever extent artists dwell on negative thoughts & pessimistic conclusions they are not being artists. In my own field it is widely rumored that film, this thing we all love & depend on, is dying & will soon be gone. It's already virtually unaffordable. This breeds paralyzation, cynicism, identification with jobs, general inactivity. It's easy to find excuses not to do work, thus intensifying social problems breeding this state of despair, instead of seeking, fighting for solutions. Sometimes in unguarded late-night conversations a quickly suppressed intimation is tentatively offered, a suggestion that perhaps something new is in the process of being born. Something better. More immediately pressing concerns are rapidly restored to consciousness & this development is left to invisible technicians in California or Cambridge or Japan. More hardware for people with too much money to not know what to do with. Progress begins in the head, however, ultimately having little to do with equipment or grants or institutions or journalistic attention or family life or fashion or personal habits or public opinion. There used to be an activity called avant-garde art that was wildly experimental, shocking settled sensibilities as it smashed citadels of opinion & taste, destroyed outmoded conceptions & institutions even, forging highways of possibilities through unrecognized wildernesses. There is little taste for such disorder these days. It's unsettling to corporate planning, threatens lifestyle. It's not hip. Avant-garde film especially is not hip. What's hip is 'Post-Modernism' where everything is phony like we like it. Be true to your TV. One hit makes a superstar & the photographers & video take over, so forget the second record. An addict population is easily forced to accept more & more cut. Imitations of imitations of imitations are sound investments. What is going on good? We need to project our minds toward future solutions to get us out of this dilemma & on to the next level. It'll be better when it's all digital, but we already have our minds. We probably have more of them than we will by the time it's generally affordable lasers. Isn't this what we've been trying to do? So what have we left undone?

I can think of a few films I haven't made. Back in the late 60's I responded to an ad in AVANT-GARDE magazine & ordered the ESP SAMPLER, a tasty LP with one-minute selections carefully edited for sequence & transition from all the records on the notorious ESP label (including Sun Ra, the Fugs, Albert Ayler, William Burroughs reading NOVA EXPRESS, Patty Waters Sings, Sing-Along-in-Esperanto, etc.). I listened to it every time I tripped. This document, along with a screening at Bestoink Dooley's downtown Atlanta theatre of Andy Warhol's NUDE RESTAURANT with Taylor Mead & Viva & a book I had documenting several performances of the Living Theatre, Allen Ginsberg via TIME & LIFE & the FILM CULTURE interview with Harry Smith, formed my image of downtown New York life. I dreamed of a movie version. Finally a movie I could see over & over. I always thought every movie I saw was either too long by two-thirds or only a tenth long enough. Movies were usually a big disappointment, especially compared to promises imagined from looking at the pictures in the fan magazines. Getting excited & getting ready to go was most of the fun. It amazed me people who went to see them more than once, what emptiness & disillusion they must carry around to return to the scene of the betrayal.

Repetition can be comforting, though. *Gratified* repetition. I used to have a collection of 45's that I played over & over, but of course the visuals were my own, or there were no visuals. In a way the whole MTV thing is a real drag, even if it did seem exciting when Bruce Conner & Kenneth Anger first did it. Sync-sound performance footage, maybe because it just shows the production of the sounds without trying to glue any meaning onto them, seems to hold more promise, even though over 99% of it is totally worthless. It seemed to me that what little there was of value could be brought together in an interesting way. The great thing about 45's was that they encouraged a concise statement. For whatever reasons, there's maybe less than 1000 hours *total* of the great jazz musicians on film. If we pick a cut-off year, we have a finite set to work with. Looking through this collection of footage, it would be clear to any filmmaker what portions don't work as film. These could be immediately eliminated, leaving us a much more manageable set to deal with. Now that all we have is relatively good footage, with a wide range of surface values, we might take an extra-filmic point-of-view & bring in the history of jazz to create priorities & categories. We might take Monk in JAZZ ON A SUMMERS DAY & cut out the cutaways to the sailboats. This would leave us with a collection of sync fragments with set intervals of emptiness between them to be filled in with other sync fragments rhythmically & otherwise matched. There only exists one short film clip of Charlie Parker, the greatest improvisor of all. That would have to be looped throughout our film to give his due share of presence. Repetitions of the same fragments would register different every time depending upon what surrounded them. Ellington was relatively well documented throughout most of his career. This footage could be arranged in time sweeps. If you have a reel-to-reel tape recorder you can sit down right now & intercut all of the different versions of "Take the 'A' Train" or you could line up a dozen turntables & do a live mix (you could do this with a dozen different orchestras playing the same Beethoven symphony). New groups could be created: Louie Armstrong with Milford Graves on drums, sax trade-offs between Coleman Hawkins & Ornette Coleman, etc. There could be a definitive 4 hour version & an avant 30 minute version.

Or we could take Marilyn Monroe. We start with everything left of her on film & eliminate all scenes where she's not on screen (except Richard Widmark in NIAGARA proclaiming, "I'm a neurotic"). This gives us a more or less approachable amount of unedited footage, a set of fragments from which to compose. We can create catalogs of her gestures & movements, color schemes by clothes or by filmstocks, she can mature & grow younger, fuller & thinner, a narrative monologue could be constructed from her language, etc. Or we could distill her ultimate image through extremely rapid intercutting or superimposition or perhaps after we work through the footage one special shot will reveal itself as containing this essence. Or we could take all of the Warner cartoons as a finite set. These could be arranged to reveal some pretty astounding insights into the modern psyche even if we deleted the obvious racial & sexual stereotyping & overt violence. Or the history of pornographic film, intercut for movement, 20 cuts per thrust, classified by sex act, by body type, by emotions expressed or evoked, etc.—the ultimate fuck.

The *entire history of film* could be viewed as a finite entity. From the filmmaker's perspective there is almost certainly only a few thousand hours of footage that is valuable as film. There must be some teenage genius out there in suburbia already at work on this project on the family's two VCR's, bootlegging bits of thousands of titles from the local video store. Such condensation & arrangement would force past footage to comply with our present needs, instead of being like the goldie-oldies stations that keep playing all the same old bad commercial shit that we hated & rotted our minds the first time around. It would constitute a renewal of the footage, place adequate value on our time, &, by example, improve the quality of new footage being shot. Since all footage carries the mark of its moment in history (the viewer can almost always recognize after a few seconds the decade a film was made: there is a 'look' created by the kinds of stocks available at the time, the deterioration, etc., just like with cars), we can undertake a huge Proustean editing project to redeem past time: the Encyclopedia of Film. This may well be the way films are viewed in the future when all recorded images are digital & mobile. The editing function will evolve into the writing (it's already very much like writing) of programs to creatively access & arrange selections from the vast libraries of moving images (Vertov's "Factory of Facts"). The concept of literacy is already being radically redefined. This could be easily extended to live broadcast & might be essential to keep informed of what's being beamed-up on the multitude of signals that can be dished out of the sky in the near future, presenting incredible interactive possibilities: Artists' World TV. All of us plugged-in together. This selection & arrangement could be according to preselected theme or it could be a composition whose combinations create new information.

Experimental film has been a tool for expanding vision, the kind of intensive viewing that it demands & develops creating new conditions for evaluating the normal bulk of moving images to which we are constantly exposed, for looking through the deceptive surfaces & examining what kind of message is actually being put forward. Which is usually buy, buy, buy, kill yourself & kill a peasant who might be a commie, everybody be the same. Viewing experimental film should be like working-out: if your eyes are sore afterwards you know they're getting stronger. I once spent a year working on a film where a number of scenes were occurring simultaneously, not through superimposition but through an alternation of frames which stretched persistence-of-vision to its limit. I found this limit at normal projection speed to be twelve, i.e., if a frame from a scene recurred twice in a second, a continuity of progression was perceived. An interval greater than twelve frames gave the impression of complete discontinuity, a rolling effect. I also found that with the continual use of the same interval (say, four frames alternating forward ABCD/ABCD, where A = frame 1/scene 1, B = fr 2/sc 2, C = fr 3/sc 3, D = fr 4/sc 4, A = fr 5/sc 1, B = fr 6/sc 2, etc.) the dominant impression was of the interval, thump thump thump thump, rather than the image. By constantly varying the interval between three & twelve (two scenes only produces a kind of vibrant superimposition effect), a hypnotic nada trance state is avoided & careful unblinking attention is encouraged & rewarded with a multiplicity of transformations, a 'dynamic geometry'. Kubelka's SCHWECHATER explores this idea thoroughly within the limits of an extremely narrow set of images. There is certainly enough rhythm going on in such a work for it to hold its own as a silent film on a program of sound films, but the question of what kind of soundtrack there might be which added-to rather than subtracted-from the energy of the piece is compelling. I wanted to make a sync-sound version, three to twelve scenes occurring simultaneously with their sync-tracks superimposed. There would be a logical relation between the sound & image, the sound being actually generated by & recorded simultaneously with the image as it was shot. I carried out my silent experiments on an optical printer, frame-by-frame refilming footage that had been originally shot normally & frame-by-frame backwinding for multiple passes, an extraordinarily tedious process. With a camera that was capable of bi-packing, a looped matte which was clear on the frames to be exposed (ten such mattes would be necessary) & black on the other frames (blocking the light) could be run through the gate along with & in front of the raw stock being exposed, greatly speeding up this process as the footage could then be combined (& the order possibly altered) in the A/B-rolling (which would, though, involve a lot of mechanical splicing unless you went to ABCDEFGH IJKL rolls). This rapid alternation of images (partially chosen for the interactive patterns they can make), whose own sequential pattern constantly varies, whose intervals (how many things are going on at once) are also constantly changing & thus also the density of its superimposed sync tracks, would be explored in all possible variations to the extent that interesting results are generated & then composition would be carried out on this material as if it were normal daily rushes. Like most special effects, this could probably be done automatically in video on a computer. Video right now, though, is so ugly. Will it ever be capable of reflecting the crystalline clarity of work like Ernie Gehr's? One could imagine speeding things up & instead of 24 frames-per-second having 60 or 1000 & then how many scenes could we train ourselves to register? By hooking up your PC to the channel-changer already you could even maybe make watching TV somewhat interesting. I have also thought about the possibilities in extremely long shots, say a 400 foot single take (approximately 12 minutes), a good double feature for the above. Lots of boring films used to be made like this, but it could be interesting. The main problem is that if everything doesn't work out, for whatever reason, the whole shoot is shot. Very costly. This is the kind of film the Pentagon should fund. The camera could be handheld & constantly moving. The perfect way for a dancer to make a film, to examine their movement inside-out. For my own work, it is likely that I will continue developing the line I have been exploring through my last several films.

Most films made have been to some degree collaborations. If you want to work on a certain scale & make original footage, it takes more than yourself alone to hold things together &, insofar as another is involved, there is necessarily a degree of input. Griffith & Bitzer & Lillian Gish, Eisenstein & Tisse & Alexandrov, the Kinok's 'Council of Three', Fellini & Nino Rota, Godard & Coutard, George Lucas & Pat O'Neill's former Cal Arts students, etc. This has not generally been the case with experimental filmmaking, where the artist attempts to work like a painter or poet, though it's hard to imagine Stan without Jane. I wanted to bring some of the energy I was receiving from other fields into film, specifically poetry, improvised music, & dance. Two works were particularly present in touching & reinforcing developing ideas for my own project, John Zorn's 1981 recording ARCHERY (Parachute 1718) & a book called LEGEND (L=A=N=G=U=A=G=E/Segue, New York, 1980).

LEGEND is made up of a series of collaborations between five poets of my generation (Bruce Andrews, Charles Bernstein, Ray DiPalma, Steve McCaffery, & Ron Silliman) & includes a 100-line solo by each writer, every possible combination of two & three, each with a unique set of rules of procedure devised by the participants & composed largely back & forth through the mails, & concludes with a five-way free-for-all. A virtual encyclopedia of experimental writing techniques, the assembled whole presents an almost novelistic unity. I'm not sure if any of the authors, at this point re-monad-ed, are completely comfortable with the results, it continually borders on being out of control, but for the reader there is a feeling of participation, a rawness that encourages similar play. I don't know of anything comparable in film, maybe ENTR'ACTE (though this is generally listed as a work by Rene Clair, he never did anything on his own of similar weight, but I guess he held it all together). It's fun to imagine possible collaborations. Experimental filmmakers, though they make their works entirely on their own, tend to have highly specialized skills towards which their works are dominantly focused. Certain filmmakers we think of as primarily editors, others primarily as cinematographers, some focus on innovative special effects, some on dramatic lighting or complex soundtracks, some are theoreticians drawing our attention to aspects of the medium we had never considered, others are great actors, all are incomplete. If a group could band together to share their skills in making a feature & one-up Hollywood on its own turf, they could make enough money to support Anthology & the Collective & Millennium & Film-Makers' Coop & Canyon & the San Francisco Cinematheque forever. This would be something like uniting Europe.

What interests me about Zorn's compositions is the attempt to establish democratic procedures through which groupings of eccentrically individualistic musicians & sometimes other artists can make coherently structured spontaneous productions. A whole movement has arisen in music devoted to collective improvisation. Players drawn from bebop, out jazz, new music, rock, folk, funk, surf, sculpture, punk, latin, neo-ethnic, classical, & others uniquely odd to start with, with an emphasis on the visual quality of the performance & low-tech homemade & prepared instruments & a demand for constant inventiveness, frequently unite in varying combinations to create a great deal of moment-to-moment excitement. The success of these sessions relies heavily on enthusiasm, chance, & a complexity of emotions. Though over the years an apparent vocabulary of signals has arisen to encourage restraint & bring the pieces to generally satisfying conclusions, there isn't consistently a sustained sense of development. I can't think of very many leaderless records. Zorn's own playing on duck-calls & multi-reeds, underwater & muted & modified by cupped hands, exposed knee, tennis ball, etc., begins by rejecting everything normal or popular, then pushes marginality through to the other side where the accepted & unquestioned unveil themselves as arbitrary & deranged. His score writing, however, is supremely rational, at least the idea of it, filling a gap so obvious it's a wonder the problem was not adequately dealt with decades ago: the possible extent & implications of the emancipation of the musician through the universal availability of recordings. This places players in a position traditionally open only to writers. The rise of home video may offer a similar opening to moving image makers. ARCHERY presents some obvious parallels to my own efforts. Here we have a document preserving historic samples of the work of a diverse grouping of artists displaying their unique tropes, but at every point the signature of the author is also prominently evidenced. I recorded sync-film documentation of the premiere performances of two other Zorn compositions, CROQUET on March 5, 1981 at Soundscape, & TRACK & FIELD on October 8, 1982 at Roulette.

Moments of these were woven together, often as punctuation, with other preserved & created performances. Through weaving I made MONEY. These included a collection of typically unusual movements enacted on the streets for me by choreographers Sally Silvers, Pooh Kaye, & Yoshiko Chuma, which I post-synched animation-style to magnetic constructions assembled from left-over music track, cutting the sound to 'hit' at points which emphasized subtleties of inflection in the movement. After working with actual sync over a number of years it became easy to create its illusion. By the time of the concluding shoots of this 2–½ year project I no longer had access to a sync rig & filmed even the talking parts with my wind-up Bolex, recording sound wild on my Sony TCD5M, & it would take a sharp sound-editor to figure out which scenes I did this with. I even reshot earlier portions of the film that had been originally filmed in sync but whose image I had lost interest in compared to more recent material which had been preinformed by the emerging shape of the final product. Real sync doesn't 'hit' at all points, so the dance footage often became ultra-sync. Other footage included David Moss singing to a Sunday crowd on Orchard Street, Tom Cora playing cello on the Brooklyn Bridge, Arto Lindsay in the basement at Georgio Grmelski's (Zu), jam sessions at the legendary Studio Henry at One Morton including the Toy Killers' playing-with-fire act, Fred Frith & Derek Bailey upstairs from Beulah Land, Skeleton Crew at the Public Theatre, Sally Silvers on the Intrepid, Zorn at his blackboard.

In PLAGIARISM, my first sound film, I had consciously lifted lines & structural devices from Hannah Weiner's LITTLE BOOKS/INDIANS (Roof, New York, 1980) & Bruce Andrew's R + B (Segue, New York, 1981). Though MONEY contains fragments from NEVER WITHOUT ONE (Roof, New York, 1984) by Diane Ward, SPLIT THIGHS (Other, Dorchester, Mass., 1976) & VITALS (unpublished, 1982) by Alan Davies, & THE FOX (United Artists, New York, 1981) by Jack Collom, I had moved away from filming poets reading their works (too little eye contact, too much object) & employed them spontaneously generating dialogue in increasingly frenetic street situations on the Lower East Side, Canal Street, & 14th & Union Square. It has been suggested that this put them at a disadvantage in relation to other artists (& this certainly was true in the 'live reenactment' after the film was done), but in fact public reading is a secondary activity for writers anyway. Poets are the conscience of the art world, because it's impossible, no matter how successful they become, that they can ever make any money from their work. Society has traditionally awarded them pariah status because of the inherent threat in the nature of their expertise, control of language being central to the maintenance of power. Avant-garde filmmakers, as the moving image increasingly supercedes the written word, have attained a similarly glorious position, even worse because our trade is so expensive to carry on.

MONEY starts over black with a disembodied complaint: "I don't have enough money." What could I say new about this topic? In the Reagan-era it particularly weighs down our dreams. I wanted to address current concerns, however obliquely. A tinkle on the cymbal, a bowed wail on cello, & the anarchist, after a glance at the camera, hurls his Molotov cocktail. An oriental woman screams & the titles begin to roll. See acknowledgements. Black again, four beats, & the text begins. The large bold Helvetica type throughout this book presents the words from the soundtrack. If you memorize them before seeing the film, you might have as pure an audio-visual experience as you would if you didn't know English. The reduced computer print-out on the left side of the pages contains the working record I kept of the shots from which I composed the film in the order I pulled them & how they hung in my trim-bin (the Wordstar file name was 'Moneybin'.) These lists are dated, so the thorough student can trace the growth of the work decision by decision as shots entered & exited the bin. The graphics are reduced xerox copies of the actual pages these were recorded on in my notebooks. All photos are stills from the film, except the back cover which is me directing the performance at Roulette. The normal sized Times-Roman type is an interview I edited out of 15 hours of taped one-on-one conversations with members of my cast. Making a book is not as much fun as making a movie, although cut-out & paste-up is a somewhat similar activity. The film is also available on videotape.

The type this size is footnotes

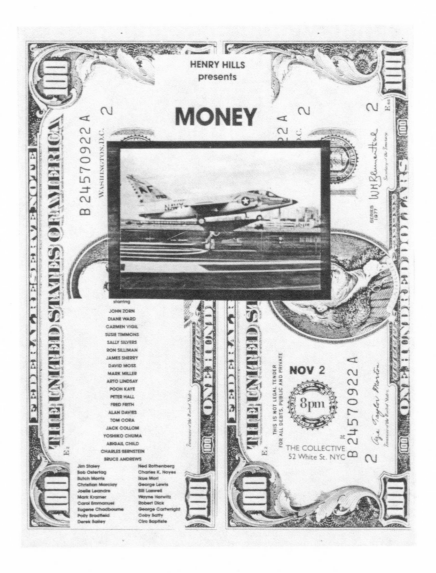

HENRY HILLS
presents

MONEY

starring

JOHN ZORN
DIANE WARD
CARMEN VIGIL
SUSIE TIMMONS
SALLY SILVERS
RON SILLIMAN
JAMES SHERRY
DAVID MOSS
MARK MILLER
ARTO LINDSAY
POOH KAYE
PETER HALL
FRED FRITH
ALAN DAVIES
TOM CORA
JACK COLLOM
YOSHIKO CHUMA
ABIGAIL CHILD
CHARLES BERNSTEIN
BRUCE ANDREWS

Jim Staley
Bob Ostertag
Butch Morris
Christian Marclay
Joelle Leandre
Mark Kramer
Carol Emmanuel
Eugene Chadbourne
Polly Bradfield
Derek Bailey

Ned Rothenberg
Charles K. Noyes
Ikue Mori
George Lewis
Bill Laswell
Wayne Horwitz
Robert Dick
George Cartwright
Coby Safty
Ciro Baptiste

NOV 2
8pm
at
THE COLLECTIVE
52 White St. NYC

11

Carol Emmanuel

I HEAR MONEY!

. . .ISN'T MONEY, IT'S THE *COST* OF MONEY

Cleaning starts the day: immaculate rollers, spotless heads, tidy bin = organized mind.

November 26, 1982

ALAN (1st)

2 1/2'	to tongue tip/runt thumb/ pre-ore/spittoon
10"	erratic spectacle (radio) (2 sc.)
10"	mistake (radio)
10"	thin.(radio)Stone--
10"	crisis(radio:93) de-
22fr	disco machines
20fr	ss(radio: dum dum dum)
15	ss asshole
13	torp/hm
11	fact
10	moss
9	ti-tah
9	rap
8	pussy

DIANE (Or)

1'	is the same thing as religion
10"	attitudes towards women
10"	more tensely then finally
10"	Think of this as a party
8"	all that noise
17fr	she's never
12fr	wan' us t'
9	really
8	y'know
9	ass(2)
6	a(ss)(1)
---	I hear money!

RON

1'	Watten (pause) ya know
10"	led directly to the assassi(nation)
9"	& it will in fact
22fr	when I saw the rushes
20fr	about their position
20	(mumbles--girls dressed as Statue of Liberty)
15	would work well
15	I just decided
14	this
12	a nice young
13	began
10	wha-doobie-do (fast)
8	(shaking kids hand)

snd only(38fr): isn't money, it's the cost of money!

ALAN (Or)

7"	unimaginable
7"	it's probably linked to the...
18fr	it's a rather long...
17	& remaining
15	(incomp; hand on head)
4	(close-up "" "" "")
14	would be rather
13	(laugh--2 sc)
13	P spoke M (guy in pix pointing at camera)
12	plastic
8	(2 sc--close face:1.glum, 2.smile)
6	to-tah
14	sis again
7	-ain
10	against
10	again
8	again

COLOM

1'	which I'm slightly vague about
13fr	Cut off my/
9	hit me
---	enough
---	& everything
---	the cars
---	scam/the sonuvabitch/scam/ all fucked up
---	say they got drunk
---	$200,000
---	was only
---	nerves

(yoddles)

CHARLES BERNSTEIN: As usual to work with you I'm supposed to come up with things to say out of whole cloth, to simply make things up which are never frantic enough for your particular moment of revelation that you would like. Your blank stare, just as in this moment which duplicates the moment of your filming, prods one to say something outrageous or something even the slightest bit engaging to say & yet there never is anything to say because you provide no content, you give no direction, just your stare & your smile & then the kind of gesture of, "Oh, more so." That seems to be one of your big ones: "More so." But more so of what? One never knows & so I'm kind of catapulted into a frenzy of emptiness & pure gesture, which, of course, is quite decadent. But as it's recontextualized by you in the film, of course, you redeem it & reconstitute it as being something interesting. But this itself—this is what you call an interview. You haven't said anything. An interviewer is supposed to ask very specific questions.

HENRY HILLS: Well, but, um.

CHARLES: Do you see my role in your films as being the same character in the three films that I'm in?

HH: Yeah.

CHARLES: And how would you characterize that role?

HH: The narrator.

CHARLES: The narrator in the marginal sense of a superfluous narrator. A narrator of film to which narration is held in disrepute. The narrator of a ship's voyage from the point of view of the narrator being on the dock and the ship is out there. It's like the narrator of the Circle Line ship but he stays at the port at 42nd St./12th Ave. while the ship is going around Manhattan but the narrator is still at the dock the whole time narrating the voyage not knowing anything about what actually is happening, which of course nobody knows. It's all constructed after the fact of shooting on 86th St.

HH: Yeah, hopefully downtown next time. Well, is that objectionable?

CHARLES: Not at all. Of course it's your work. No, I mean, I've always discussed in the films this very topic. I'm simply continuing almost a running dialog which I've had in the three films of which this could be a 4th instance, about the nature of appropriation of—I wouldn't be so much interested in the films if you didn't in fact deal with the material that's presented & use it in some way. In other words, if you simply left the stuff that happened in so-called 'real time' be reproduced this wouldn't be interesting at all to me.

E-yun-doc

HH: Although that's still there, you know, it might be interesting in viewing the film to try to reconstruct. . .

CHARLES: . . . what this other, but the reconstruction that you would do of what the original thing would be like a 3rd thing. There might be what the actual original situation was like, then there's what you've done to it, & then the possible reconstruction of the original would be even further away; that would be even more of a fantasy or projection. You'd get further away from the so-called reality or historical fact of the filming by this 3rd level of reconstruction of what it must have really been like, because it wasn't *really* like anything.

HH: Just me saying, "Oh, start talking."

CHARLES: Yeah, I mean, there's the talking, there's the film & so on. There's so many different elements, that what actually occurred is so already screened & delimited by what you actually shot in the first place, the way in which you shot it & how the interaction of the camera & the being-filmed & the way the spectators & the situation responded to the fact of filming—all of these things altered the situation & made it into a kind of nether situation that wasn't ever quite what it seemed to be even at the time. It never was & never will be. These're only possible constructions, such as the one that you make with the actual film, such as the one the viewer might make in imagining what it might have been like, but it wasn't *like* anything!

the, the RICH

```
11"     uh systems
10"     like totally the opposite
 8"     where it's all different
18fr    editing people
23      their styles
19      Broderick Crawford
16      systems
11      systems
11      systems
```

December 1, 1982

ALAN (1st)

```
10"     mistake (radio)
10"     thin.(radio) Stone-
10"     crisis( " ) de-
21fr    ugh sighs
15fr    flesh
15      ss asshole
13      torp/hm
13      (wierd eyes, snds like:)
        love
11      suction
11      fact
 9      state
 9      rap
 7      verb
 6      call
 5      get
 3      mick
```

ALAN (Or)

```
21fr    situation sss
19      that this was
16      (mutter mutter) shit
15      (incomp)(hand from head)
15      ___spoke___(guy pointing
        a camera)
13      (laugh--2sc)
15      & dreaming
12      luckless
12      (hand patting head-2sc)
12      plastic
11      against (not a)
11      means only
 8      merging
 8      yes
 9      Alan
 8      (laugh)
 5      touched
```

RON

```
 1'     Watten(pause)ya know
23fr    socialist society
21      isn't in control
19      uch is one reason
16      I've gotten a lot of
15      like choosing
11      to within
 9      so
 7      writing
 7      top
 7      writing
 7      has a
---     will in fact
```

DI(Or)

```
 1'     more tensely than finally
22fr    (can) never remember
        his name
20      retaliates
16      feminist
18      innocence (noisy)
15      (i)s based on--
13      this woman
13      she what she
12      careless
13      & also
12      spoke
12      album
10      toe tuh
10      liquid
10      flesh (2)
 9      flesh (1)
 9      over
 9      a little
 8      I guess
 8      to stop--
 6      verb
 4      punk
 4      punk
```

DI(resync)

```
24fr    you walk away
18      etc
13      right?
 9      grab
```

DIANE(2)

```
10"     get everyone together
        like
23fr    (shaking head)...yeah
22      writing is never
23      why what?(pause)(1)
18      yeah (pause) (2)
22      when he looks
22      well, yeah, it does
15      were doing that--
15      oh (blush)(pause)
15      that's what I hate
```

&, uh, my mind* goes ♊ on (off)

binary, dialectical even

HH: What do you feel your role in MONEY is?

ALAN DAVIES: I'm a figment of your imagination. Briefly.

HH: What about the way I dealt with your work? I plagiarized it & made it my own, right?

ALAN: No, I thought that was just a form of articulation. At base, all use of language is plagiarism, right? Y'know, plagiarism from the mother & the father & whoever you learn language from.

HH: It's hard to talk about your work, right?

ALAN: For your work as a filmmaker, you mean?

HH: For anybody to talk about their work, because you're bound to have more thoughts about, I mean you're constantly thinking about it, so at any given moment you're only going to focus on the ideas that you have at that moment, whereas you have a constant flow of ideas about it the whole time you're making it & from then on.

ALAN: & before. Well, that's why people keep notebooks, I think, in part, is in order to maintain some kind of control over all of that stuff that goes into the making of a work. I think that that's a quality that your film has—by virtue of the insistence of the quantity of the cuts it contains the way that it was made, so you don't feel that it's just like a product. You feel that the process of making it is also there & also a part of it & in that sense I guess it contains also its own critique or whatever might happen after the making of it. I think that that quality in the making of the film is one of the things that's most likeable about it & most generous really. It doesn't feel like it's put forward as a product of work, which it certainly could because of the enormous amount of work involved, but it feels really like it *contains* that work & isn't a representation of it or even a container of it but the work is still there. But as far as any role in it, I don't know, I mean, it's the world, but I thought of it as a kind of like flat presence. It's similar to the way you think when you pose for a photograph or even when you suddenly become aware that somebody's taking a candid photo, somehow always in my mind & without any process of thought, it just kind of makes everything feel flat, everything suddenly feels two-dimensional & I think that's why people sometimes don't like having their photograph taken.

* "I don't have any, haha"

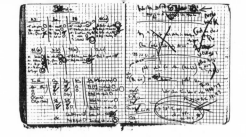

I'm remembering money.

Sounds like: Capitalism. Debt. Caniption fit.   HIT ME!
It's kinda caniption on the grandparents. Bebop. Bizarre. Chaotic. Whatever sync robots, upper-middle-class, Christian, whatever the Soviets.

```
15        (shakes head no, soft,
          pretty)
14        describe
13        direction
13        (laugh, pigeons
          descending)
13        (laugh)
14        process
13        no (childish)
13        to the next
11        (interesting pale face)
12        ---I don't know---
11        verbal (or 'movement')
10        always on
9         point
8         point

          YOSH

10"       (cut-up!) nnn (4th St)
17fr      (snds like:) let's get it
          on
13        takey-a-munta
12        ahhh (4th)
11        moe-TOE
11        (breath) mmmm (4th)
9         canicut-tuk (fast)
8         hush-she
8         tay-ky-de
8         kvaa
6         kiddido
5         (w)aah (cheerful)
5         a-ha-te (breathy)
5         ssk
5         coo-coo
10        ahh (4th)

          JAS

20fr      buying & selling
18        feeling terrible
18        pleading with him, said
13        you're drunk
13        was
12        flay-us some
9         next to the
8         could say
8         saying
7         in this
7         film
7         to
7         to go
13        more money
MONEY:    9, 9, 7, 7, 7, 7, 6, 6

          CHAS (2)

22fr      the verbal & the visual
18        interfering with the--
15        kilter
14        uh...oh
14        versus
14        sequence
12        the image
12        the noise
12        upon a (1)
5         a (2)
12        so that's what
10        or
9         vision
8         (man walks by, Chas. looks
          insane) click/gulp
7         (laugh)
7         bones
5         why
4         sss
5         (pix only--Chas. looks
          crazed)
```

POOH KAYE: But let's start with where we turned on the tape recorder which had to do with people being uncomfortable about being taped or being filmed, cause I think that people who do it regularly for a living have a method of relaxing the subject.

HH: I have another bottle.

POOH: Oh, good. You know that they really, when I've been with people who are very used to, especially like photographers who are very used to photographing subjects, they really can make people, they have a way of like talking a person into, beguiling a person, seducing them into a kind of ease as if there were no barriers of self-consciousness between.

HH: Well it's different though with film & with photos. There's nobody in Western culture that won't accept having their photo taken, it's just like a part of—

POOH: No, most people are uptight initially.

HH: Uptight, but everybody has their photo taken a few times in their life, but whereas being on film—somehow that's more revealing.

POOH: Cause they can see them moving & they move *ugly*. I don't know, I'm pretty uptight about being photographed & I'm pretty uptight about being filmed & I'm pretty uptight about everything.

HH: About being recorded.

POOH: Right & it takes somebody doing some kind of seduction, emotional seduction, to get me past that point where I'm aware that there is a medium between myself & that person. I think that's part of being a voyeur of any sort is this ability to break down a barrier, that's part of observing, whether it's through speech as a journalist or if you're looking through a camera, I mean if that's what you're looking for, if you're looking *at* the world through your exercise, I think you owe it to the world to try & make it as easy as possible for it, like getting me drunk.

TIME   (to-tah, ti-tah)   **$200,000**
would align us poor   (toe no toe)   **in the heyday.**
What do you want me to ?

Dec 12, 1982
JAS

13fr	everybody's
11	and
8	(laugh)
8	ssss
7	that
7	money
6	down
5	so
5	& the
8	film
6	money

ZORN (on st.)

13fr	what it means (1a)
7	(snort) (2a)
8	about
7	I thought a- (3b)
9	tonight? (2b)
4	what? (1b)

CHAS (2)

---	---bones
14"	I don't trust the camera (cut-up!!)
10"	physical eye sense
13fr	uh-oh
13	oh (pause)
11	in-a
12	sight
12	(speeded-up funny)
7	stop
7	ho
6	I mean
6	year
5	po (1)
5	po (2)
9	ss(ho) o
15	--you might say

Yosh/Colom scene: yoddle/take-i-munta

DI (2)

7"	I know Henry always--
6"	(3 sc--movement)
18fr	which is interesting
15	were doing that
15	next time
14	language
10	(laugh)
11	(snds like) verbal
10	& up
6	(speeded up, overexp, in front of gunshop)

DI (resync)

9"(2sc-guy going in door):partial	(you walk away)
	(grab)
19fr	(mike click) relax
7	flow

AL (1st)

17fr	could last
11	(crazed eyes)
10	ass
9	purpose (n)
9	screw (v)
6	ak
4	can
4	-t
4	per
4	bly

AL (Or)

22fr	analysis of this (again, / again)
9	someone
8	remote
8	last
7	cock
7	said
6	in your

DIANE WARD: I was totally surprised by it. I mean, I don't even remember saying all that stuff & to see myself on film is very strange. It's like totally unintentional everything in that film that I'm involved in. It was just like rambling & sort of being there & running around on the street with you with all this equipment & everything, & that was enjoyable, I sort of enjoyed it, & laughing with Charles, so that then seeing the whole film later, I was just this background thing to like the invisible big idea which was you making the film, so that you were very present, I thought, & then everybody on the film was sort of in the background. The film precluded everything, overshadowed everybody, the fact that you made it & the process. So that's the whole exploitation side of it, right?

HH: ?

DIANE: Because you're so unprecious about it. You're not like preserving everyone in some sort of typical time structure. You don't leave anything alone, so that way there's no great value put on a person's personality and their actions. They become these visual & sound elements, but isolated & not really attached to the real world too much. They're like very frantic & very kind of distressed, I think. Excited. Traumatized.

HH: It's more like lighthearted in a way, isn't it?

DIANE: There are elements, a sense of humor, but not always. Sometimes things are very poignant & sort of sad.

HH: Sad?

DIANE: Yeah, there are moments like that. Just the whole attitude about taking something & cutting it all up is like nervous.

SUSIE TIMMONS: Well, it's all right. It was fun to do, it was interesting to do it, I had big circles under my eyes, it was fun. It was hard to watch the movie & not feel narcissistic because all I really cared about was how I looked. I had those glasses, so it was nice to have a record of myself wearing those pointy glasses because I'll never probably ever have those again, y'know & that was sort of a thing & I feel like that phase is over. Last winter was terrible, because I started out, I had Unemployment in 1983 till September & then it ran out & theoretically I was gonna get a job the minute my Unemployment ran out but it ran out in September & I didn't get a job until like December, then I owed like $1700 & I had like a Dispossess Notice & everything, I was really just destitute, then at that point my laundry, I left all my dark clothes in the laundromat at 13th St & A & I went away to get a newspaper & a coffee or something & I came back & the man had taken all my clothes out & lost them. Like all my dark clothes.

. . .led directly to the assassinat—/uh, it, I. . .

It's probably linked to the digital crisscross action around the figure-8 triangulation scene, right? More Oedipus.

```
        DI (Or)
---     (more tensely than
        finally)
11fr    yourself
12      organize
11      (good backgrounds)
10      of which
8       tenses
7       (speed-up) was
8       repeat
4       aa (abyss)
---     punk/punk

        RON
12fr    one's self
10      control
8       incomp
7       but our
6       play

        MOSS (Or)
---     (jar) 13, 9, 7

        COLUM
---     (yoddles)


Jan 3, 1983
        RON:
20fr    (very speeded up, ends
        "city")
12      one's self
11      workers
9       apart
9       broken-up
8       (incomp)
8       muscles
8       today
7       men
6       to do
6       play
4       lip

        MOSS
(jar)(Or)....
(tin)(Or)....
(drums)(Roul)....

        DI (2):
3-4'    is ,um, vague, is very
        vague, is not, is nothing
        in particular
16fr    because I hear it
15      were doing that--
15      next time
11      (not loud, snds like
        "verbal")
10      (laugh)
10      and up
6       (speeded up & overexp)*

        COLOM
"hit me" & yoddles
```

HH: You have the title role.

JAMES SHERRY: I should have been on stage a lot more. My role in the film was a kind of punctuation, except in the "Money" section of MONEY. You forced me into this.

HH: You're the only one I knew that had a suit.

JAMES: Basically I thought the movie was a counterpoint thing, juxtaposing say Sally Silvers to John Zorn, who were really sort of the stars. The real meaning that comes out of the film is the sense of its masses, not in the sense of its timing or the overall line. You can't concentrate on it for 20 minutes & get a sense of trajectory, & since there's no narrative, you end up having an accretion of these little focal points.

More "G.L."

HH: But as you become more familiar with the film. . .

JAMES: After you see something a certain number of times then you're no longer getting meaning out of the film. You're putting meaning into the film. I think what really gives shape overall structure is repetition.

HH: Oh, to say that life has structure is just to look back on it. Like it doesn't have any structure as its happening.

JAMES: Individual events in the immediate sense. That's an interesting question. I suppose they do by virtue of the fact that you never exist only in things as they're happening. You're constantly classifying things & remembering & projecting & saying, "Oh mv God, if this person reaches over & kisses me."

Bruce complete soundtrack:
   "So we're walking around imitating this criss cross action around the figure-8 triangulation scene, right? More Oedipus, more R.K./translations, more greed, more Graeco-Roman. You want the old wrestling style? You want the new wrestling style? We can break into the energy fields, ya Henry? I/ . . . he's not, however; he's a businessman trying to sell *you* everything he can sell you/comedy, we got imposs-/," etc.

Bruce Andrews

"E-o-wanna kick-kok-tic," or even *cured:*
a future existence in Outer Space.

```
YOSH:
screams
1'          day wanna kick cock tick/
            day bah
12fr        coocoo nina (Av A)
11          kinah (hands in pocket)
            (4th)
8           tugo djun (4th)
8           kvaa (4th)
6           kiddiddo (Av A before
            dance)
5           (u)ahh
5           coo-coo

            CROQ:  (misc)

            T&F:  (misc)

            T&F:  (Zorn)

            ARTO:  (u Zorn)
                   (solo)

            CHAS (2):

---         (I don't trust the
            camera:Cut-up!
13fr        oh (pause)
13          ah--ah
12          sight
11          (lost in serious thought,
            truck passes)
11          in-a
7           ooo(ahh)
7           ho
7           bones (high!)
7           stop
6           year
6           I mean
5           po (2)
5           po (1)
            kilter

            JAS:

22          so (pause--hand goes out)
13          everybody's
11          trade
11          and
11          uhh
8           (laugh)
8           sss
```

SUSIE: You know that thing of seeing yourself is fun, first of all, & it's very primitive. I always think I'm funny about it, like I'm funnier than other people about my image. In my family no one ever took pictures so every time I see my picture I'm always intrigued by it. The first time you watch the movie that's all you're looking for, y'know you can't even enjoy it because you're just waiting to see what you look like. So then you're there & you see yourself & you feel very nervous because everyone is there sitting next to you *seeing* you too. So you wonder how you look & you sort of look not so great. I felt like sort of spotty & big circles under my eyes. Then the 2nd time you see it it's nicer because there's all these people in it & you're curious to see how they are & what they have to say & I couldn't understand how they fit together in a certain way & that was very interesting to me, I hadn't considered our proximity.

POOH: ...but it's not like a big ego display. I don't feel like I'm like, I don't really think there are any stars. I'd say all of the people in the film are doing weird things & saying weird things.

HH: Somebody pointed out that you were the only one who doesn't speak.

POOH: I know. I wondered about that. I felt a little hurt.

HH: This person thought that that made your role much more mysterious & interesting, because of the major characters you were the only one.

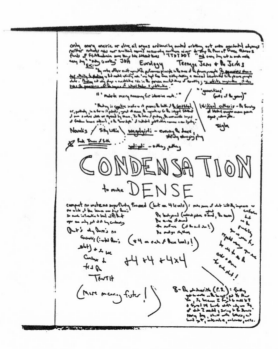

"-oic"

Ha, ho, I see   that a greater menace . . . You don't know.
I thought artists belie work (which isn't too clear) & I think that
(blank!) that they got, that their TRUST NOT PERISH.
   It's this security, perhaps, of-of-of swerving breasts that
they need   (much more rapidly)   all the time.

   I don't!   don't want it!

```
7        that
7        money
6        down
6        money
5        in the
5        so
4        ssss

         DI (Or):

12       organize
12       space
11       yourself
11       splice
11       (good background pix &
         snd)
11       for me
10       of which
10       moments
9        forest
8        (speeded up) was
8        repeat
5        this
5        you
4        aaa (as abyss)
4        punk
4        punk

         ZORN (on st.):

3'       the man is across the
         st...
26fr     ooo/(whine of tin)(nice
         jumpcut)
9        tonight
7        tell you
7        I thought a--
4        what
3        (thump)
```

JOHN ZORN: I think that I'm in a lot of the film. I kind of see myself there, but maybe that's because I'm looking for myself or notice myself easier or I'm self-conscious about seeing myself.

SALLY SILVERS: Well, I mean I'm in there more than anybody else, right? You let me say a lot of cuss-words mostly & I think it gives a really good indication of the type of language I prefer to use & my attitude on the world. Um, let's see, & I like the movements I was doing then. It was really a long time ago though, so those things seem more like ancient history now. I mean they're very clear to me what they are, I have them written down.

BRUCE ANDREWS: I'm just curious, other than the kinship thing, why not just use trained *actors* or TV personalities or people that are used to reading the news or people that are used to speaking in the classroom or giving talks before social service workers or people that are great storytellers, raconteurs, or something like that?

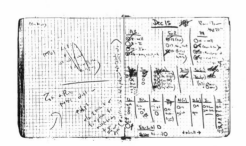

Ron Silliman

Um, a little more sudden, old, didalittle pecker (HIT ME!) State direction interfering with the remote control role analysis of this, y'know, I don't know, y'know, anti-Socialist society, the verbal & the visual, & the hideous attitudes towards women.

ZORN (in apt):

27fr	a bit of a wierd head
17	situation
16	get involved
13	everything else
11	system (under breath)
9	like maybe
7	piece

((music))

SALLY (Rafiks):

1-1/2'	(blink)as a whole it's totally fucked
14"	(pause-eyes) was all
36fr	papers, remember?
35	you know, (haha)
29	(pause-eyes) to stop
28	& then have you release it
26	(breath) oh boy!
16	don't sync up
14	as it is (snotty tone)
14	really shitty
14	decide
13	you just want me to--
13	moving
13	I mean women--
12	area
12	very vary
12	(laughing)-they're gonna get
9	things
9	(laugh)
9	what is
9	workers
8	workers
8	film
8	digital
6	but
6	women
5	women

(SALLY, Jan 10):

24fr	why isn't it functioning?
17	capitalism
14	(movement)
13	gimme a break
12	it turns out
11	certain things
10	with us
10	and
10	well--
9	(of) course
9	to stop
9	tension
9	voice
8	men('s)
8	uh
8	music
8	hmmm
8	trying to get
6	uh
6	writing
6	and
6	(laugh)
4	(laugh)
4	sss

(Canal St--resync):

17	otherwise
13	ha, ho, I see
9	well

SALLY (resync) 1-28-83:

24fr	they try to get you to feel
23	let's see
20	for years

HH: Well I think trained actors would be something quite different, but otherwise you're right. Anybody who could talk well is an appropriate choice for the role that I gave the poets in MONEY. As far as future work, there's no reason why it couldn't be any other artist who's articulate. My inclination, though, is to continue using improvised dialog.

BRUCE: Well what's so great about improvised dialog?

HH: Because I want it to be more like *real life*.

BRUCE: It's not like real life when you have people out in the street being prodded to be charismatic, moving around on Canal St. to find some exciting backdrop, where it doesn't even matter that much what the words are as long as you say them really strong or really exciting or really sexy. In real life, the only kind of dialog there would be would be at home. People *don't* stand on the street & give speeches, so what's so naturalistic about that?

HH: I've heard people stand on the street & give speeches many times.

BRUCE: Yeah, but not the people you're asking to do this.

HH: It keeps coming back to *your* feeling that it would be more effective for me to be using actors & a pre-written script to be doing what you perceive that I'm doing.

BRUCE: It's a possibility.

HH: There are other possibilities also.

BRUCE: Like Charles is a very great talker, but his talking doesn't necessarily have that much to do with what makes his writing very distinctive. My suggestion would allow a place for the poets in the future.

HH: I like to have a pretty clear vision of the finished piece before I start & structural ideas, but I prefer to let the details kind of emerge & then make the film on the editing table.

Their styles: REACTIONARY!

```
19      (light laugh)
15      (laugh & breath)
13      worked with
13      he learned the--
7       like
6       parts
6       and

        T&F turn to 45


        OTHER

Sally(Raf): 13 ha, hao, I see
Di(Or):     11 careless
Zorn(st):    9 tonight?
Al(Or):      7 said (sat)
Ron:         7 ha-ah
Ron:         7 but our ((sun
                 on truck)
Al(Or):      6 -uck M (fast)
Jas:         5 so
Zorn(st):    4 what (fast)

also       Miller
           St. Henry
           misc Sally dance
           misc Moss
           Colom yoddle
           Yosh
           I&E_____
                       etc.

March 25, 1983

        MOSS

Roulette & Roul.2(etc)

        RON:

15"     /(whao!), drew pa-
13fr    capitalism
8       in his
6       to it
6       it's the--
6       yellow
5       but our
5       feet (1)
5       feet (2)
7       to me

        DI(Or):

14      t-shirts
12      Griffith
11      careless
11      yourself
8       W
8       W
7       without
7       nip
7       and
6       in all

        AL(Or):

13      material
11      did not
10      again
9       events
9       someone
9       -atten or
7       said (sat)
7       W
6       -uck (-oke)
5       U.M.
5       wrote
4       -bly
4       (laugh)
4_____or a
9       problem
9       loss
8       release
7       crumbles
8       yes (speedy)
6       loss
5       not
5       less


        DI(2)(resync)

14      mistake
36      filming in a bar 'one
         time'
```

SALLY: We were raw material in some ways for the way that you compose, but the level of meaning that's there, as opposed to like NORTH BEACH, is on a whole different level because of the fact that you're dealing with all these elements that are not so easy to categorize. I mean you can say, oh there's movement, there's sound, there's language, there's this, that, and the other. But it's not like you could say, oh there's the lamppost or there's the stairway or there's the landscape. It has some of the same compositional techniques which definitely say, OK this is Henry's film, but the raw material is much more variable. You're composing those thoughts based on the language you received or the motion. I don't think that it was necessarily your point to clearly individualize the people that were in the film, so in that sense it's *not* a documentary. It is & it's not at the same time.

HH: Well I thought that *by* the way I put it together, it was emphasizing the interrelatedness of these different groups of artists' aesthetic concerns. The interaction among this group of people has increased over the time I was working on the film. I mean I saw certain connections with people who weren't really familiar with each other's work, but have become & even have collaborated.

POOH: Right, now I'm working with all of them. It was prophetic.

HH: The reason I thought to do this book is because the film finally is so short that in the kind of context that normally you have the opportunity to show your films, it just goes by & it's just another film & it's more than 2 years of my life but it's just 15 minutes of the audience's life & most people might normally only see it once or twice & so I thought I'll use all the excess stuff & monumentalize it more than just a 15 minute film which is maybe very interesting to whoever might see it, most people I would think, but still it's just like a little short. Most people engaged in a 2 year project would probably make a *feature* & I feel like as much work & as much thought went into it as a feature-length film & certainly as many scenes.

ALAN: The only real difference is that it didn't cost as much.

HH: Although it cost quite a lot for a film of that length. And it's still costing!

SALLY: In a feature you're not that conscious of the editing. I think most feature films are planned so that you don't notice the editing so much. It's supposed to have more of a natural, it's supposed to be more like what you experience in actual time, even though they cut back & forth to past & future, there is more of a sense that you're really existing in that time frame.

. . .ahhh & it, I don't know, OK, retaliates.

HH: But that's such bullshit, because it isn't at all like what I experience in actual time.

SALLY: Well would you say you experience what your films are after 2000 hours of editing or whatever?

HH: Much closer than a Hollywood movie.

SALLY: Come on, man, you're a laid-back kind of a guy, y'know, you don't sit around your place or experience your life events as this fast-forward, multi-focus, incredibly stimulating environment. I mean you have to make that, you have to make that happen.

("(local issues)/into the city")   as fast as it possibly can go!

MORE MEANING FASTER

HH: You don't know how I experience when I'm sitting around, but certainly like when you go out on the street in New York it's like that. You constantly have multiple demands on all your senses that are constantly pulling your senses in every possible direction & so your consciousness is very fragmented as you're walking down the street or in the subway, just being out of your place in N.Y., I think, not when you're in a movie theatre when the lights are off, but if you're at the Collective with half the film community there or when the lights come up at DTW or Danspace when every other dancer in N.Y. is there, your consciousness is going to be pretty fragmented then too, right?

SALLY: Um hmm, especially if the piece is bad.

HH: Well, if it's good, that's because *it's* fragmented & it's taking you along on its own fragmented course.

SALLY: Exactly. I think there is a natural *developed* inclination towards fragmentation when you live in an urban environment & when you have these options of choosing what's gonna affect you or not, when you're walking down the street you *don't* have those options, so that, yeah, you're inclined towards seeking those things out after a certain point, I think, if you become urbanized or if you live in some stimulating environment like this, like N.Y. And so if you don't get it in the piece, yeah, look around the room or you're gonna get out your paper & start writing stuff or your mind's gonna wander onto things that you'd rather be thinking about. Yeah, you're gonna make that happen for yourself in some way.

That's what I hate

HIT ME!

12	presses her
8	(closes book--at end!)
7	debt (speedy)
7	lies
7	-ped kit-
7	wild
5	self (fast)
5	pft

SALLY (resync)

26	great (pause)
24	(laugh) I--
20	for years
19	(light laugh)
13	he's learned the-
14	working
13	worked with
13	(2sc) parts/like
7	fail
7	y'know
6	and
12	class

SALLY (Rafiks):

24	why isn't it functioning?
13	ha, ho I see
12	very vary
12	area (flashbulb)
11	certain things
10	and
10	make-up mirror (hands)
10	well----
9	don't you?
9	(laugh)
6	writing

ZORN (home, talk):

17	everything except
10	systems
7	kind of a
7	piece

EASTER

June 17, 1983

CHAS (LES)

1-1/2'	(1) communicating emo-tionally one to another
2'	(2) & one can feel free to express one's emotions
32fr	(1) this is all being, being
1-1/2'	(2) interplanetary starwars
36fr	vascular coagulopathy
23	people interacting
22	monosyllablic
13	that a greater
9	y'know
31	wd you give me $2 (Br(Can)15fr:$2.50,2.7--)

HH: I find that even in a completely rural setting also. It's like in a suburban setting is where you have this big void; then it's just your TV set & your car & the shopping mall.

SALLY: Yeah, well, that's like the leveling of consciousness.

HH: It's like preparation for colonizing other planets. You just won't be able to open the windows of your car because it'll be pressurized.

ALAN: Well by making the book it's sort of like if you take the size of the film in terms of its temporal duration & posit that in relation to the amount of your life that went into it in terms of temporal duration, what you want to do by making the book you're trying to give people something intermediary. You're giving them a book that would take them say 2 hours or 3 hours to sit down & digest. You're trying to somehow fill up the gap between 15 minutes & however many minutes there are in 2 years. . . Get out your calculator. So you're disappointed, so you want to have a stepstool that people can get on. They still won't be able to see over the edge into what your life was like during that 2 years, but at least they'll realize, it'll push their realization into that direction, maybe. Well look at this thing that's been on television the last 3 nights, HOLLYWOOD WIVES by Joan Collins, right? I mean, I don't know how long it took her to make it, but it's precisely the opposite ratio. I'm sure it didn't take her more than 2 years to make the book & yet instead of that effort telescoping down in terms of temporal duration to the 15 minutes that it takes each viewer to see your film or ½ hour if they see it twice or 45 minutes if they see it 3 times, y'know *millions* of people have watched this 6 hour extravaganza on television, so it's as if the whole audience for your film walked 180 degrees around & while they were going around the half circle, consciousness or like the world situation or something took out your film & put in this Joan Collins film instead & suddenly they're looking instead down at this little kind of minute thing. I think the book's a good idea in its own right, no matter what. You could make a book now, after making this book or instead of making this book, about a film that you haven't made.

Well, I don't know. You don't know, though, y'know, & that all our energies exist towards PROCESS.

Let's see:

Arto Lindsay

Sally Silvers

John Zorn & Tom Cora

David Moss

It's the self, they get feet area in all tension, kind of fun, sort of (fuck him!) more complications threatened. Go now, y'know, so. . .

CARMEN

30fr	I don't think I could take that
26	uh, when I have some money
22	that's 10 ft (use to indicate piece exactly to the frame 10')
18	trying to get money
14	(laugh)
11	some money
10	around (2)
9	around (1)

SUSIE T:

2-1/2'	& a youth gang is approaching with baseball bats (parallel to Zorn: "The man...")
2'	(pause) the only thing ...THE ONLY THING--
31fr	you don't know, though, you know

HH: Well I thought I could use the interviews exactly like I made the film, y'know, cut them up & make a composition out of that & not even bother trying to . . .

SUSIE: . . . trying to find a way to keep it in some kind of order, I mean I've never really developed any kind of actual system. I'm so fraught with disorder & disorganization & *that's something that has a lot to do with money*, because this is the first time that I've ever had time & money & that's what it takes to get organized . . . just doing all *that* takes time & you can't be worried about whether you're gonna have money for dinner or not . . . I read a self-help book called GETTING ORGANIZED & that was very useful.

Right? Go he-dough, even though events come just by to it, yourself did not. I've. . .

30	when its not so well
29	and there's the river
24	(pause) I guess
23	why
21	incompetent
18	a certain kind of---
16	(laugh)
11	uh-ah(hh) ( )
11	media
10	sounds like
13	or something

ABBY (LES)

11"	Charles, ha, ha
10"	as fast as it possibly can go
22fr	G.L.
29	(consciously representative (close -up)
19	(laugh)
21	20%
17	that's true
16	the make
15	female
15	energy
15	DOWN
15	down
14	(r)roll
13	(laugh)
13	ahhhh
12	too. (or 2.)
11	pft!
11	joker
10	I don't know
10	ah-ah-ah (light)
10	yeah (parallel to Di2 'yeah')
9	sort of
9	(laugh)
9	(laugh)
9	so little
8	go
8	go
8	(incomp.($))
7	building
15	with a lot of-
15	complications
13	late enough
11	stroke
8	to
6	but
8	they get
6	hmmm
6	the

ALAN: But it makes a denser experience if you tie it even hypothetically or randomly or even with an effort at obfuscation, to the actual details of the film script, not that it's a *script*, really. What would you call it? It's not like you scripted it in advance. The 'trace.'

HH: Well, I have it written out now.

ALAN: Yeah, but it would be very difficult to take it out & make a film using it & would certainly be impossible to take it out & make the film, or anything remotely like the film that you did make, using it.

HH: Although, the performance at Roulette . . .

ALAN: See what I mean. The performance was like a garment that the film had worn for a long time. Like a sweater that the film had worn through an entire season or something. So that it had . . .

HH: A few holes.

ALAN: & odors, certainly, & lumps here & there, but it still kind of retained the shape of the body. Also it was larger, it lasted longer, it was larger than the body. It was sillier, too.

Filming in a bar one time, I thought, "Screw Pa! This is all being, being realized *not* to sell you a certain kind of, uh, y'know, CAPITALISM VS. WORKERS in interplanetary "Star Wars," right?

I gotta fix my hair.

```
          ABBY (Canal)
1-1/2'    respond to it, react to
          it
28fr      /girls kicking
30pix,26snd(4fr more pix at head)
          (incomp)
21        talking
20        or an indian
19        don't want it
18        da-ah-ah*
16        robots
15        wierd
15        society
13        (laugh)(dark pix)
12        this show
9         will do (2)
11        will do (1)
8         (incomp)
12        um
12        anyway
5         beep

          BRUCE (Canal)
4'        "so we're walking around
          imitating this criss-
          cross around the
          figure 8 triangulation
          scene, right?  More
          Oedipus, more----"
31fr      (pause) Blakean Godhead
26        cause that's what we're
          here for
25        we don't have time to read
24        it's all available
22        well, I don't know
          ((outrageous))
21        what the fuck do you
          think
20        it's not gonna cost you
17        what's possible
16        OK
16        conniption fit
10        (incomp)
8         right?
8         y'know
8         more (1)
7         right?
7         right?
7         a little more
6         Hills
5         right
9         energy
9         so
7         right?
5         more (2)

          BRUCE (resync)
16        thataway
13        romantic
13        mummies
10        noise
10        fun
9         off
7         do you?

          SALLY
dance w SH3 quartet (snd=1',
                    pix=7")
26        great
24        (laugh) I----
20        for years
19        (light laugh)
16        (oriental dance on
          stairs resync to Croq)
13        ha, ho, I see

          POOH

          YOSH (2)

          MOSS

          ARTO

          ST. HENRY
```

ZORN: Well, what about the performance that you did? How did that relate to the film itself? When you were putting the film together, did you have the performance in mind? When you were putting the film together, how much did the words? The words kind of become sentences; you took a word from one person & a word from another person & you create a whole different set of meanings & the whole thing 'money', there's a lot of stuff about money, people are saying, "money" & not just Sherry but a lot of people, like a lot of references here & there that kind of tie the film together *thematically*, but how much did a real kind of narrative sense play in your construction of the *ordering* of the separate shots? I mean there's lots of ways you can put shots together. I mean, one way is by taking a word from this person & a word from that & then it adds up to a sentence or a poem. You're doing it kind of by meaning or you do it by sound, you want sound splashing back & forth in a musical kind of way, or visually—you want a very dense shot, then you want a single-person shot. What were your criterion in picking shot after shot?

HH: Well, I wanted all of that . . . I mean, I would start each editing session by doing pulls & I would go through my different material which some of the shoots were aimed towards getting language & some towards music & some towards dance & pull shots out & put them on the bin that holds all my elements that I compose with that night & whatever was left over from the previous nights & I had this bin full of shots arranged in various categories, so I would get warmed-up for 4 or 5 hours just pulling shots, which is a big part of the composing anyway because as I pulled the shots I would pretty much plan where they would begin & where they would end—I would choose out the frame that they would begin & end on. I would like look through my rushes & some scene would strike me, either I was looking for certain types of material for one reason or another & then I had categories, whatever was useful at the time for storing the pieces in the bin. After a number of hours I would start putting the pieces back in & some days my head would be completely into working with the language & then other days it would be more with the music, but it would have to always work rhythmically; even if it worked as a sentence & the rhythm was not good then I recomposed it until it worked both ways, & *then* I would have to see how it worked with the other stuff, so when the sentence worked for the rhythms & not with the music then I'd have to stick music in between, little bits, weird things would balance it off. Sometimes putting a whole hunk a minute earlier of something else would just change the sway of the whole piece to where something much later would work. Whenever I find myself working in the next room from someone who works in the industry, I'm always amazed at how homemade & raw

Think of this as a party. The male got drunk, y'know. What the fuck do you think? Erratic spectacle! (like totally the opposite) Unimaginable! Nerves!

```
                 T&F
Zorn    "tonight?" 9fr
Jas     "so" 4fr & "asses" 11fr

                 AL(Or)

6fr     -uck M
5       U.M.
5       wrote
5       less
        --again
        --against

                 BAILEY

        FRITH(only)&F&Z(Ave.A)

        FRITH(only)(Roulette)

        JOELLE & TOM

        SKELETON CREW

        YOSH

27      oh dose wahwah (A)
22      e-o-wanna-kick-cok-tic(A)
20      (sync dance, cellar
        door)
11      day-bah! (4th)
8       (sync dance, 4th St)
8       (resync) to know toe
7       (resync) uh
7       (re) he-dough
7       (scream)
4       (scream)
11      (re)dzou-k'nee
11      (re)neek-STAA

        COLOM (yoddle)


June 29, 1983

Frith & Joelle (1)
Frith & Zorn (5)
Bailey (1)
Br(re) off ()
        thataway ()
Br(Canal) "Hills!" ()
        Blakean Godhead ()
Abby(Canal) don't want it ()
        respond to it,
        react to it ()
Abby(LES) joker ()
        too.(2.)()
        with a lot of--()
Chas--that a greater ()
Sally--(laugh)
        for years ()
Al(Or) U.M. ()
Yosh--to intercut
Arto-------(3)
Yosh (on bench) ()*
Yosh (on swing) (6)
Pooh (truck) (5)
        (other) (4)
Sally(dance) (5)
```

my methods of working are, being kind of invented as I went along to accomplish what I needed as the problems arose, like I might be the supreme expert in certain narrowly defined areas & not even have a beginning film student's knowledge of other basic standard procedures because the necessity for that solution never came up. If you question the validity of the majority of movies made, I mean there's a lot of work involved in even making a piece of shit. I totally respect workers. Sometimes people are amazed at how many splices I made & that it's all clean & A/B-rolled, but just think how many a professional negative-cutter does, and what does that mean? I mean, when I first saw experimental films I found the grittiness & scratches & watermarks & glue drips & fingerprints & all particularly attractive; they focussed me onto the surface of the film, made me aware of the material, opened up a whole new way of thinking about the possibilities of film that Hollywood had never offered, dramatic results at a millionth the cost, but when I began making films, I saw *my* work, initially at least, as a way to make some order out of my life, as a discipline. Obsessive precision & neatness, hardly a hallmark of my daily existence, assumed an integral role. I wanted to present totally out-there ideas with an immediate clarity. I look at the work thousands of times as I work so it's made to last, so you can look at it over & over & keep seeing new things. I like to keep the action going on lots of different levels. Why should movies be any less dense than real life?

ZORN: So it was more your intuitive way of putting it together than some kind of set formula?

HH: Right. I mean I had systems for how I would work with it & how I categorized & pulled shots, & I had them all logged. I worked certain things out on paper, but it was basically intuitive. And, once I got going on the project, my shooting was governed by what I needed for the editing.

Which is interesting (mmmmmmmmm) Which is one reason to stop & I don't wanna.

ZORN: It's a really long process. I mean it took you *years* to do it, right, so over the course of years each time you'd go up there it's kind of like you were inventing new systems & playing little games with yourself.

HH: Right, exactly. I filmed you talking about TRACK & FIELD when you were still finishing composing it on the board (& I filmed T&F's premiere at Roulette later) & I broke it up as I was shooting it, which is what I did all through this movie; sometimes I wasn't even listening to what people were saying, I would just be going for visual stuff & then work later with what I got. That way I wasn't so stuck with what people happened to be talking about, but could rather explore *how* they talked. I got the idea for the performance before I finished just because I had generated a lot of notebooks of material & I wanted to do something more with it. I had the cue-sheets for my sound-mix with all of the words to identify scenes on that & the relationships between the periods of music & the periods of words & I just sat down in a couple of nights & wrote the score based on that, so structurally it would parallel.

ZORN: The feeling of it wasn't like the film, but there were elements that were. I thought it was interesting, the relation of what the performance was to the film. At first I thought, well y'know he's not really capturing the film at all, the speed of it & then you want the text to come through & then I *realized*, I'd seen the film several times but I never realized how the text had woven through to create almost a narrative & how there were pieces of that & how that was fragmented. It seemed to me the first time I saw the film you were just dealing with the images & the rhythms, rather than taking words that were important to you & putting them together to create another level of meaning that the film really has. I mean the film exists on so many levels & when I saw the performance I was aware of several other levels that I hadn't been aware of just seeing the film. So I think the performance was very successful in that way. It was kind of like A SKELETON KEY TO . . .

HH: Exactly . . . And as far as 'money' went, y'know, I never have a title when I begin or if I do, every time I have I've changed it at the end, like every sound film I've made started out called MARXISM AND FORM. Maybe 6 months into the project when I put together one of the early versions of it, it started off with that line where Diane says, "I hear money," & it's really funny because what was interesting about that shot initially was that by some weird coincidence she said that & right at that moment this cash register rang out on the sound, but it was like the sound quality of the system I was using is so bad that after editing for a while *that* completely dropped out & I lost it forever, so my main decision for choosing this shot was totally obliterated, but it was also kind of central, because I had had no money for so long & then suddenly I had a grant to make the film & then I spent it all & then I had no money again, y'know that obvious thing, provocative title for grant applications or whatever, but it wasn't, I mean *for me* all of the language doesn't center around money.

ZORN: Enough of it to kind of make it present in someone's mind.

HH: Well like somebody was even relating your scene with 'The Man' to money.

ZORN: What a great scene. Horrible! God, I look terrible in that movie, I think, I look so stiff. I really don't think I'm very comfortable . . .

BRUCE: But there's something about the film being called MONEY & some of the elements in it that suggested that you were moving towards more thematic coherence around a topic.

Well, it's sort of one's self so being able to position
(put. . .PUT)   traffic so that   ("oh GOD!")
the cars

HIT ME!*

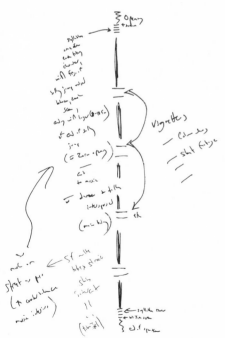

HH: OK, well in that sense, I wanted this *line* that was supposedly telling something about a topic going through it, but I wanted constant detours. When I was trying to work out the overall structure for this piece at a very early stage in my notebook ((see left)) I was thinking about this Melville story "The Encantadas" which is kind of like a miniature MOBY DICK where it has some kind of story that weaves it together, but basically it's a whole bunch of chapters about a whole bunch of different topics, it's like turtles instead of whales, but the thing was you could draw a diagram—this one thing going forward but there were all these little pockets that were just very slightly related to the line that was moving forward, these kind of unified periods of interruption, & that's the way I thought of the structure of this piece. This money theme is always kind of moving it forward, although I don't know that it moves forward; it just keeps coming back to it, but it's always going away from it too. I thought of MONEY, although on the one hand it is centered around this one thing, I thought of it on the other hand as a more encyclopedic work, that it had a form that could incorporate more kinds of things or at least it presented the possibility of a form that could incorporate more kinds of things than any of my previous films.

ALAN: Yeah, it's encyclopedic in its ability to include, its willingness to include. It's like a history of N.Y. art consciousness, at least during the years that you made it.

BRUCE: Why was that? What was it about the form, why was it different from say RADIO ADIOS in terms of being able to incorporate more?

*Fucker, they're gonna!

Rode on out.

torsion

HH: Well RADIO ADIOS had this one line that just continued all the way to a certain point & then it stopped & then it started up again, there was like a coda at the end.

BRUCE: Not a thematic line.

HH: No, it was a line in the sense of one thing led to the next thing to the next thing to the next thing smoothly without anything interrupting this. Maybe there were references to earlier parts or whatever, but rhythmically & the way the words fit together it kept moving forward in one continuous monologue—I mean there were some parts when it was a dialog for a minute—but it was basically proceeding along, whereas MONEY I felt like, not only did it have places where I was interrupting the line more but it also had these pockets where I would have a hunk of something else that was discreet. There were scenes that only appeared once, instead of being cut-up throughout the thing.

Shout: HIT ME!

BRUCE: Well that might have something to do with the thematic focus too in a way. It might be that having a little thematic focus enabled you to feel much freer about breaking up the linear progression.

HH: & digressing into any kind of area that I feel like.

BRUCE: Right, because you knew that when you came back, you would be coming back to something that had a coherence with other things that went before, whereas if there's a whole variety of different types of thematic material, then you have to kind of work it into a single linear progression & you have to be very careful then about when you stop it & when you start it up again, because you're depending on a *line* to give it coherence, whereas if you depend on a *theme* to give it coherence then you don't have to have a single line, you can have this scattered thing going all over the place. With poets, they sit at a desk & you write a poem about a theme, something's on your mind or some mood you're in, I think it ends up having that thematic focus *as well* as having usually a kind of linear progression, because of the fact that it's all being composed at one time & to me that ends up seeming too limited. I get bored with that. It's like redundant. To me you need the line, some kind of single progression, *or* you need some kind of thematic focus, you don't need both, either one is sufficient.

Out to strain retaliation.

July 21

        RON
15fr   away from home
11   perish
8   function (fast)
7   to lead
7   pen
6   eliptic (speed)
6   I wrote (speed)
5   not
4   not (speed)

        TOM
        (Joelle) (2)

        ARTO
        (Zorn) (8)

        COLOM
        (closes book)
        (yoddles) (5)

        ABBY (Canal)
1'   girls kicking their legs
19fr   that they got, that their
15   focus that way
15   my mind goes
14   but just coming
12   realize
11   Hi!
11   (incomp)
10   wait-a-minute
9   s'kinda
7   OK
6   (laugh)
5   (laugh)
5   / (movement)
5   oh
4   / (movement)
        ((free pix))

        ABBY (LES)
15   with a lot of
14   would align us
12   uh----
11   wait-a-minute
9   (pause) I think
8   come
8   definitely
8   home
7   to be
7   down
6   towards
5   come
--------- ((free pix))
12   too*
11   joker**

        BRUCE (Canal)
10"   conniption...the
        grandparents
18fr   to sell you--
17   beneath me
16   operation
14   in the heyday
14   you, YOU
12   now
9   energy
7   right?
5   right?

HH: Well maybe that's true. Anyway, I felt like in some ways just financial limitations kept that encyclopedic aspect from being more stressed. If I had been able, at a certain point in the filmmaking, to shoot more footage, then it would have had more variation. This also exists on the level of lengths. These fast scenes are flowing together in a rhythmic way & then there's these interruptions where there's these long scenes, like for instance I would have liked to have had a lot more long scenes in the movie, but if it's like a hit-or-miss kind of thing you gotta shoot a lot of footage. When I finally got some more money it was beyond the point where I could start adding all this length to it.

SALLY: . . . & then you want to go on because you don't want something to overlast what it needs in order to be what it is. You have to assume people are paying attention & that they want to be stimulated & that they're going to be bored in that 10 seconds or 4 seconds or 2 seconds of lag is wasted time for people cause people don't mind wasting time as long as it's their own, but when they're looking at what you're doing it's not their time really.

ZORN: It's a really *organic* way of working, it really makes sense. I really admire people that have got their own mechanics down. This is a completely integral way to work. It's perfect! It makes me think. Like the way you're working with film, it's like it's fantastic, it's incredible. I mean it takes you a long time, but it's perfect. I think it's a perfect way of working. You can't go wrong. It's gotta be great. You start, you build, you build more, you build more, a little bit at a time, stick something here, something there, it's getting bigger & bigger & bigger, keep putting little pieces, it's fantastic. And like the way I work with my pieces, the rules, I think that's perfect. It's a perfect way to work. It's got so many ramifications & so many levels & the same way with the way you work, it's got so many levels to it & it's so deep, you know what I mean? You can't go wrong. You've been working for all these years, right, & now you've got it down to a science, that's kind of what it is. You've got your language together, you know what you're doing, you've got your way of working together. That's like magic.

"to tongue tip / runt thumb / pre-ore / spittoon"

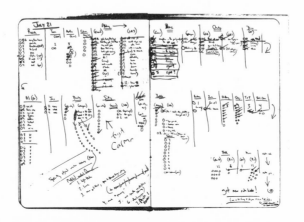

HH: I feel that what I'm trying to do is explore possibilities that exist in film before film disappears. It's inevitable. It's such a backward thing in a way: y'know this mechanism based on the bicycle, this chemical thing that whatever it takes to make it pollutes the environment.

PETER SEATON: What if it disappears before you're ready to stop making films?

Broderick Crawford

HH: It's not going to disappear until it's replaced by something that's seductive enough to make all the filmmakers quit making films & start doing this other thing, right?

PETER: Including you?

HH: Especially me. Like digital, I mean like this bookshelf could have like the whole New York Public Library on it. It just seems only completely logical that they will eventually have some kind of electronic thing that will more than compare, that will be *lots better*. Why not? And not only would it look better & be much more vast a thing, but also you'll have access to even more minute pieces of it. You have access to every single point. Instead of having access to frames, you get access to every single grain within every single frame. You'd have so much more control than you have now, I think. There was this article which I read a few years ago in *Fortune* magazine, my father cut it out for me, & said, "This looks like, I think you'd be interested in this," y'know, & it was about *imager chips*. Y'know they have chips that hold the information in computers but they also have, or they're working on, chips that can *see*.

PETER: What do you mean? That can—

HH: Can *see*. My impression was that it would be like these little tiny eyes that can see as good as the human eye could & give the same kind of information to the computer that the eye gives to the brain, but they would be like a grain of sand, so you have this wall & instead of having one lens focussing on something forcing the whole audience to more or less look at the same thing—I mean on a big screen you can look all around the frame & stuff, but really you're more or less focussed in a certain direction—if they had this thing that was like 100 billion eyes on this wall here looking at something, then you could have like millions of perspectives on what was being filmed & the editing possibilities are *amazing*.

```
                    (resync)
15fr      process
12        things
16        thataway

          AL (Or)
13        exist
11        that's nice
11        against
10        again
9         sudden
7         listened
5         then
4         or a
---------------------
8         W
8         W
8         W
---------------------
6         P
5         P
5         P
5         P
4         P
4         P

          JAS
11        asses
10        where
9         are

          POOH
(pix only) (4)
(resync):
          box=10
          truckbed=10
          other=4

          SALLY
(pix only) (8)
19        (light laugh)
20        for years
6         and

          YOSHIKO
(pix only, new) (7)
(pix to intercut w old) (7)
(resync) (6)
(talk):
1'        comeda step, sheddita ma
          (background noise!!)
8fr       dzoy-k'noo (resync on
          Ave A, 2nd shot)
          yo-qui-e
          coo-coo nina
          kenah
          day-bah
screams:  7, 6, 6, 5, 5, 5, 5, 4,
          4, 4fr
```

& there's the River

(thud, thud, "ko guy pa," thud)   DA AH AH, you might say,

ABBY CHILD: We're talking about it like escape or daydreaming, but it's also control, so that it offers you actually a vision of control in a world that seems otherwise uncontrollable & the word 'control' or power has this double-edge to it. Is it control in your dark corner, control of a margin of the world? Or is it control that somehow will *affect* the world, which you hope for actually?

HH: That was the whole thing about daydreaming, when you make art you kind of rein in that impulse, instead of just letting it freeflow all over everywhere, & also you make it into something concrete. By making this thing you take your fantasy life & make it actually change the world.

BRUCE: So what role do you think this film might have in the revolutionary transformation of the advanced Capitalist society? That's a rhetorical question. I think it's important to raise that though. And how you think your future work is going to be even more relevant to the struggles that are engaging the world at this point.

HH: I need closer access to the pause button.

"Scam / the sonofabitch / scam / all fucked-up"

ALAN: What do you think is the most *obvious* feature of the film?

HH: To me?

ALAN: Yeah.

HH: Well the aspect that I enjoy of it is the density of the movement, not only the movement from scene to scene, but just within the scenes there's so much density of movement, which is kind of a development. Like in PLAGIARISM there was pretty much not too much going on in the background. I was just filming people reading & talking, nice backdrops but I kind of began to understand that what was interesting me was when other things were going on behind as kind of decoration & I did more of that in RADIO ADIOS & in this one, where I allowed myself a huge shooting ratio, I totally went for this kind of, plus I became much more uninhibited about going out in crowded situations on the street to shoot to obtain that kind of imagery, but who knows what if I look at it in 10 years I'm going to feel. I can't say that at this point I see things I've never seen, but I get a huge amount of exhilaration at all this wiggling around in the rear & one leading to the next & swirling motion. I guess I could take it much further even, & eliminate all the foregrounding. There is still pretty dominant foregrounding from one person to the next even though all this other stuff is going on.

35

It's a rather long operation.

ALAN: There's also foregrounding of other aspects, like the sound. I.e., you could create it almost entirely in terms of rhythms & gestures & stuff & just have this incredibly flowing thing, sequence of images.

HH: Without any language at all.

ALAN: Yeah, without any attention to language. It would limit the kind of humor that you'd be able to permit or the kind of contradiction or the kind of repetition of vocal elements. Although I think you did an incredible job of mixing those different aspects. There are times when the discourse appears to be swinging in one direction & the movement appears to be going in another direction or through that dimension. I mean I can imagine you taking that & saying, alright forget the sound, I'm going to edit just in terms of movement, but in the film you actually manage to have elements & aspects of that while at the same time you had literal statements made by a group of people in sequence, or a non-group, a sequence of people in sequence. You would see people kind of contributing to this on-going mini-non-statement, at the same time that they were doing that you might have also found gestures that followed one another either in terms of coherence, meaning that the 2nd gesture that occurred followed through from the first, or in terms of contradiction in that one went one way & one went the other way. That's why after the film when I asked you how you did it, y'know, which of the things was most important, that was because to me that was the most amazing aspect of the accomplishment.

OK, what-a-be-do Soho toe to MO TO to go (A nice young Mick)

SALLY: What's carrying the load of the meaning at any given point varies, & some things seem to act as the main carrier of the meaning in a particular instance & other things seem like punctuation & other things seem like disagreements, like some kind of contrast blaring in at it, or at other points it seems more like what's holding it up, y'know like that wasn't enough so that all these things were kind of building to make that stand on its own like some sort of accumulation thing to make a particular point that you didn't know it was leading up to stand on its own. It varies how each thing comes across depending on what's happening at the time. And some things are punctuation—like big exclamation points everywhere.

HH: I feel like your work particularly lends itself to that kind of, that it is real segmented & so it really lends itself to short scenes like that.

SALLY: Well we plotted it that way too, though.

The only thing, THE ONLY THING, um, she's never some of the things you want in your film about physical eye sense tenses. (Gimme a break)

HH: You do that with your own work, right? You take these little small pieces & rearrange them & compose from . . .

SALLY: Yeah, rearrange & compose from small units. Things are tending to vary a little bit more now, though. I mean I'm not exactly doing phrases, but things do tend to vary more over the course of what they are.

HH: You're moving into your prose phase?

(great)

SALLY: Yeah. More than just one thing that repeats itself until it's made an impact, which I think was what I was mostly doing then. It turned out that doing something three times seemed to be the point at which it registered. Once it was never enough & twice it didn't seem to have enough there, enough substance, & three times—that's usually what worked. And four times it seemed like it was actually a repetition. Actually I read somewhere that Buster Keaton found that same thing. He found that anything he did he had to do it three times before it would register on film. So that was like a curious thing. I don't know whether you thought of that when you were deciding how many cuts of something to use or whether you found a certain logic as far as how many times you needed things to appear before you thought they made their visual statement in the film.

HH: I would put things in & either keep adding them when there wasn't enough or keep taking them out when there was too many of them. And so I worked with the dance movement pieces the same way I worked with the language pieces or the music pieces.

SALLY: I just found that out on my own, too, but it also creates sort of a monotony now so I'm more conscious of it. I'm more conscious of it being like a time limitation so I vary it more now consciously.

HH: Well I noticed the last shoot we did, there was maybe quite a long time between that & the earlier shoots, that there was definitely much longer phrases there.

People interacting   "Hi!"   Well, well.
. . .like choosing, building, & dreaming; talking, writing again, right?   Writing is never feeling terrible.*   Ugh!

BRUCE

26	your possibility
23	you wanna be? you wanna be? (cut in 1/2?)
19	some of the things you want
18	he's a businessman
17	beneath me (to)
16	(resync)(beep) thataway
16	whatever the Soviets
14	by, you want a little
12	now
11	actually
10	what it's gonna
9	sync
8	mind
6	work with
5	/ (hands)

ABBY (LES)

38	went home & I almost went immediately to sleep
13	member
13	inhumane
12	(smile, guy walking in front, truck behind)
11	wait-a-minute
8	P
8	home
7	(movement & truck)
7	to be
7	down
pix only--	(sticks out tongue)

SUSIE T.

26	which isn't too clear
12	in a little

ALAN

7	listen(ed)
4	or (a)

RON

7	pen
7	to lead

ZORN (@ blackboard)

20	um (pause)
20	that would then create

SALLY: Plus that was improvised. The stuff we started out doing, I remember I just took my notes with me & just went down the list. I wasn't confident about doing improvising at all then. To me, in the film, the earlier stuff actually seemed more filmic, because it was, I think, more distinctly angular in some way & contained. With my own eye, now, like seeing the repetition in the film almost bothers me, because that's just the way I am about movement, I don't think it's like something in the film that people would get bored with, but for my own eye in terms of movement I never use repetition in my own work as far as going back to something that was earlier in the piece & doing it again. I mean sometimes maybe it gives a clear sense that something's been composed, instead of like a string of ongoing events. Often if you go back to something it's more of a clear-cut indication of a compositional device, the old musical ABA or whatever. In dance, too, always it was considered that was like one of your basic compositional ploys was to make a phrase, make a variation of it, & then go back to the original or whatever, not that you're making variations but that seemed to be a stop-point of indicating that you made decisions about how it was composed.

HH: It's funny cause James went into this long thing about how it didn't have that aspect to it & therefore it was impossible to feel any overall structure to the piece.

SALLY: Oh I didn't find that at all. First of all, if you're just looking at it as a moment to moment structure then that assumes that each part that you have in it doesn't have any relationship to the whole thing. The way you work, the thing takes on a shape even if you don't impose it from the outside.

Sighs want us to, I don't know.   HIT ME!

Alan Davies

A.O.K. (duh-duh-duh), so that's what ("yeah, shit") & everything began trying to get DOWN
where it's all different language or all that noise:

Disco Machines

DIANE

7   and, uh

YOSHIKO

12   coo-ka nina (Av. A, truck)
11   hinah (4th St., hands)
8   to no toe (Tompkins Sq.)

JAS

20   (9 + 11) are/asses

CARMEN

20   that's 10 ft.
15   this place

CHAS

10   (sniffle)
6   (serious look down)
     election
     bones

YODDLE (5)

SCREAM (9)

SALLY (resync)

2'   ("if you're not getting enough" etc.)*
32fr (my laugh, her eyes, her slight laugh)
28   & radical elements
22   (pause) she's out
19   (light laugh)
19   chaotic tape
17   styles
14   as it is
7   and think
7   and then
6   and

T&F (4)

Butch Morris (1)

MOSS (Roul) (3)

ARTO (2)

ST. HENRY (4)

SKEL. CREW (7)

FRITH (A) (6)

SALLY

pix only (5)
resync (6)

POOH (resync) (5)

YOSH

pix (3+1 old)
resync (5)

Sept 22 = 387 ft

Nov. 17, 1983

POOH

pix only: 15, 15, 15, 14, 13, 13,
13, 11, 10, 10, 9, 9, 9,
12, 10, 9, 8, 6, 6, 5,
5, 8, 8, 8, 7, 6, 6

synched (12)

T&F (9)

HH: When you asked me what my first perception of the work was—

ALAN: Yeah, your main experience of it.

HH: Other people, lots of other people, seem at least their initial experience of it is one of speed, which some people find very problematic. I mean this one woman in Germany posed this argument as if someone else had said it, that like this is so typical of America to do something *so fast* that it's almost on the verge of being out of control, just faster than you can possibly take in, faster than you could reflect on at any rate, & that this is connected with the Arms Race. At least it's not doing anything about the Arms Race, it's just like continuing the same kind of crazed mentality where you have no sense of any end, you're just like going as fast as you can go & just finding ways to go *even faster*.

ALAN: She must have been a Green person.

HH: But I've heard that over here too.

ALAN: Yeah, but the problem with that is that when people say that that's an expression of a personal perceptual problem, because they're caught up in a dilemma of whether this is one thing that lasts 15 minutes or 1600 things that are all packed into 15 minutes. If her primary experience had been of a 15 minute thing bounded by beginning & end that happens to have incredible varieties of texture, then she would never have raised that question. Then it would be like whatever speed it had would be interesting but it would simply be the speed bounded by that duration. It wouldn't be a statement of loss. I.e., she's saying, "There are 1600 things packed into 15 minutes. They go too fast. I can't see all of them." So her argument was as if you had made a 2 hour film but speeded it up when you showed it. It's a perceptual problem that keeps people who make that kind of response in a certain position. That would be like going to look at Hieronymus Bosch's GARDEN OF EARTHLY DELIGHTS & saying, "This is a failure because there's too much information in here." And it's really just somebody who would rather go look at a portrait by Vermeer. It's not even an aesthetic judgment or statement. People who have that response are just telling you where they are, really.

          Miniaturization, not speed.

SUSIE: Where did you say that? That was an interesting thing that fast shots were considered aggressive & masculine, etc., like this kind of cultural feminist analysis, that fast movies were masculine & aggressive & the real slow movies were feminine. That was in the program, right?

```
        CROQ. (3)

        MOSS (2)

        BAILEY (1)

        ABBY (LES)

17fr     I can't remember
 8       we are-
 5       art
13       (Can) to strain

         RON

 7       to lead
```

HH: That's not exactly what I said. There was some kind of argument that was *implied* but I never could ever see a straight version of it, but it was implied a lot of places & people referred to it, although I have never been able to find where it exists except for just by implication, that political films, films that were politically correct, were, had those *long*, slow, which is bullshit, you can't find any concrete examples that fit that, & it came up in a review of Chantal Ackerman's work. (tape break)

THIS media ass would be rather incompetent, which is kind of like the noise, ("it's hard") &, uh, something like the image upon a verb, right? Saying, "a verb," right? Could say, "Wanna cut off my.* . .?" Pleading with him said, "I've gotten a lot of. . ." (Di shakes head No) (background: "Why not?") "I just decided really, uh uh, LOVE."

It's gonna be (It's true) VISION that *this* was   (nnnn)

```
        CHAS

15       election

        BRUCE

24         they wanted the cigars
23(10+13)  you wanna be? (twice)
16         thataway
           beneath me
11         the Soviets
10         your
 8         my
 7         sell
 6         sell
 6         film
 6         akk

         JAS

10       asses

         YOSH

(cellar door)

        FRITH & ZORN (1)

        TOM (BB) (11+1a, 2a, 3a)

        SU (2)

1-1/2'     (laugh, pause)
1'         $1300, haha
9"         (laugh, populated)

         PH

2'         upper middle class,
           Christian
1-1/2'     & factories in outer
           space...studies have--
22fr       the rich people have
11         cannot
10         me
---        I gotta fix my hair
```

SUSIE: ...why is it so appealing? I mean that's the thing, there's something very appealing about the Ramones, that's the thing of speed & stuff, there's something really energizing about things that are really *fast*, y'know, almost it's not just because you have a short attention span & it encourages a short attention span, I've had that argument with Europeans about how Americans just have terrible attention spans & I'm really dubious about that, y'know, cause all that popular culture that we just eat up, everybody around the world craves, anybody in an advanced industrial society really wants—

HH: & not even, in the Third World also.

SUSIE: Yeah, right. Everybody wants that kind of patterning. It's something that's happening to you at a rate that's faster than your heartbeat. That was the Muzak definition I saw at one time. Muzak is all physiologically geared to be slower than your heartbeat cause it soothes you & if it's just at your heartbeat it makes you feel happy & peppy & you know music that's louder than your heartbeat interferes with your heartbeat & causes you to have a heart attack.

HH: I find that Muzak has the opposite effect on me. It makes me so nervous.

Editing people ("'cause that's what we're here for") was only systems, uh, monosyllabic, uh, systems   (sss asshole)

* "vagina dentata"

SUSIE: Me, too. I find it freaks me out when I know what's gonna happen & I can't hurry it up; I feel really out of control. I'm not a cultural feminist. I don't believe that certain qualities are negative & therefore masculine & certain qualities are female & therefore good. Maybe a long shot, like a slow thing, is supposed to be like sort of nurturing & patient & kind & unrushed & that has something more to do with female, y'know, sexuality, in a very direct way, it would take you longer to become stimulated & that men are rapidly stimulated & this translated into like a lot of fast stuff going on & speed & getting everything over with quickly, &, to me, something about that, there's some kind of something *missing* in that kind of thinking. How can you start ascribing a moral value to time? Like a negative value to something that's short & a positive value to something long? I think that's very strange, because the person that's doing that is saying there's a big difference in the way men see time & the way women see time, & I don't know if that's true. I think that's not true. There are plenty of differences already; that's like inventing new differences. I think you might make a male movie & you might make a female movie because of course you're seeing & things you're going to see are going to be directed & conditioned by your background & your class, your education & what you think is true & what you don't think is true & what you think is permissible & what you think is not art, that's all going to be conditioned by your background, but I don't think speed is one of those things. Also, how much of what you see *isn't* gender-based? Is your gender the *only* thing that you express when you're making a movie? If that was the case, you wouldn't be able to look at a movie that was made by somebody of the opposite sex because you wouldn't know what they were doing. It would make no sense to you. Unless you were a woman & you had been brainwashed—that's the idea, I guess, that your own values had been destroyed & then replaced with the so-called aggressive male values.

HH: There are certain values that are represented as male values that I don't accept as *my* values whatsoever, & I'm very sensitive about at what point taking people's images is exploiting them & at what point it's permissible. It's an open question, in a way, & I have to deal with it constantly. I feel *personally* responsible for the way I deal with people's images & in a way it makes it easier that I use friends, because then it's very conscious always that I *have* to be personally responsible if I want to remain friends with these people.

SUSIE: Well, in a way that's egoism; you want your friends to be interesting people. Who's that guy who took all those pictures of people shooting-up all the time out in Tulsa? Why does this guy want to show us how fucked-up all his friends are? I never knew an *artist* who was a topless dancer or a junkie & didn't tell me all about it. It's like they never do it in secret shame. It's always like a big public thing. . .

Flesh get flesh, flay us some

HA ha HA ha HA ha HA ha HA ha HA ha HA ha HA ha HA ha HA
HA ha HA ha HA ha HA ha HA ha HA ha HA ha HA ha HA
HA ha HA ha HA ha HA ha HA ha HA ha HA ha HA
HA ha HA ha HA haHA   hahah

"Right?"
"Yeah"

Charles Bernstein

Susie Timmons

Abby Child

```
          A(3)
2'        *move & talk, move &
          talk, motion pictures*
1-1/2     *capitalism isn't
          dramatic*
1'        no, ha, ha
34fr      I think all these words
          are a little...
34        I don't know, you know
          like-
31        *days, haha*
28        its only a symbol
27        (finger as gun to head)
23        & how do you deal with
          all-
22        good, good
21        *these are off*
          ((glasses))
19        (laugh)
16        bebop
16        *shout* (1a)
16        (pause) I (pause)
15        *I'm a-* (2a)
14        express
10        well
7         (close-up laugh)
          *what does it mean?*

          YOSH:  (scream) (6)

          COLOM

          (yoddle=4)+1

Di (for me)/Ron (oneself) ()

          free pix (3)

MONEY=title as of Oct, 83

Rafik sells his Frezzi

Nov 10:  averaging 10'/hr
         synching-up footage
         shot on Bolex & wild
         cassette

Tues, Nov 22:  11 min, 28 sec
         or 409 ft, 10 fr

11 pm, Dec 1:  422 ft 2 fr or
               11.43 min/sec

12:30:  426.29 / 11.51

Dec 9:

          ABBY (#3)
9"        days, haha
          (I'm a-
          shout
          ROTTEN
9fr       I
8         well
```

HH: . . . we were just talking about self-improvement, but I'd rather talk about film.

POOH: This is for your grant, right? We can't talk about the flexible & forgiving element of human nature?

HH: As long as we don't mention names.

POOH: Well I think it helps for one to exist incredibly in the world if you don't see yourself as a perfect person. For me, at any rate, I certainly was doing a lot worse, if you can feel like, well, not only are you not perfect, but also you're made of plastic materials & your possibility for assimilating new information is still functioning.

HH: I don't think it was a matter of thinking of yourself as perfect, it's a matter of thinking that your glaring imperfections were an unchangeable part of yourself.

POOH: & that you had to maintain defenses in order to cover up for your maladies. It's not like that.

HH: It is a weird thing that you can know that you're totally fucked & still have lots of ego-strength & ambition.

POOH: You can still provide yourself with pleasure. That I figure is the ultimate.

HH: Or you can still contribute.

POOH: To the universe.

ENERGY

JAMES: There's this whole series of lives that you were participating in while you were filming MONEY. The fact like that I was going through this serious illness. . . People in your films going through their lives & what was really going on in their minds while they were presenting this supposedly objective artistic viewpoint of the world.

HH: Well I filmed it at different times & I continued my relationships with most of them & still do & their lives continue to change or whatever, mine also, but it doesn't, well in a sense that did connect to the editing. It didn't connect so much to the shooting of it because like maybe I shot Alan 3 years ago or something & a lot of things happened in his life after that which certainly doesn't affect the footage I have of him because it didn't affect his being before it happened, not that he's any different in any real sense now than before.

JAMES: I think he is.

HH: Well maybe he is but the fact these people are the material I'm working with over a period of time but I'm also interacting socially with the people & my feelings towards them lots of times would affect decisions I would make in the editing for instance. I mean I might get pissed-off at somebody & I wouldn't just cut them out, but I would look much more critically at their role.

ABBY: They're all crazy as a result of the hold of money on their lives & imagination & so everybody's struggling against something that they're shaped by. My work seems to be about smaller or more intimate issues. I'm looking for areas that haven't been explored. That's one of the things in a wandering imagination that is really fertile is that you can actually permit your digressions & penetrations of convention or of subterfuge, on the other hand, to surface & be utilized. I don't think daydreaming, if it's an escape, it's an escape for freedom since most of the world seems fairly patrolled. I mean if you're talking about foregrounding of multiple points of diversion, I think that happens in your work & think that happens in my work, whether or not that's an answer to monopoly capitalism is another question, or it is not the question. Seems like maybe it's not escape but it's this sense of something that can be controlled so you film it & foreground it because that you actually registered on your brain. That incident, that gesture, that moment, that speech made a mark that you could throw back out in your art, so it's kind of like a recovery process almost, but that makes it maybe too much like memory & that can be really nostalgic & I think the kind of aggressive, what people call aggressive, rhythms in your work & in my work are an attempt maybe to penetrate the censor of convention, the censor of peacefulness.

Focus that way. ⟶

The sequence in this film is based on play, always on the innocence of mistake, broken-up space, & a bit of a weird head.

SU (2)

14"	when they decay
10"	I don't have any, ha
10"	This is my street
18fr	so/ /that
13	(laugh)

PETER HALL

1'	---alright---
1'	& I have a theory about this
19fr	& I don't wanna
15	like I l-like
9	with a little

Dec 14:

AL (OR)

against

DI (OR)

10	whatever
9	open

JAS

7	home
13	traffic

C2

13	research
16	the/the

ZORN (home)

"5 or 6 years from now" & music (2)

POOH (2) (6)

TOM (BB) (10)

ZORN (7th)

6fr	or so

SALLY (re)

1'	(my laugh & hers)
18fr	(pt2) (Ron: when to press the button)
13	chaotic
6	just by
12	(to Colom: "stinks")
15	(Raf) classes
13	(") idea (dark)

CROQ (5)

SH (3)

ZORN: Well what are you going to do next? You gonna try a totally new approach?

HH: No, no, I want to incorporate everything I've done up to now into something that looks different at least on a surface level. I feel like the form that MONEY opened up—it doesn't have to be all quick shots at all, it can have any kind of shot. I'm going to do less foregrounding & have more than one person, instead of having one person relating to the camera, for a lot of it I'm going to have 2 or more people relating to each other.

ZORN: Well when I think of a new piece, it's kind of "Well what's missing in the last piece?" So what's missing in this film?

HH: By having it be more than one individual, that opens up a lot of possibilities for framing & also. . .

ZORN: But it also brings up a *narrative* quality. Is that important to you?

HH: Well, in a lot of ways that has very negative strong connotations, right? But, well, I have a lot of trouble with 'acting,' y'know. If I could do like a narrative quality but still have it be real live people just being themselves then. . .

ZORN: I think that's what we need, I think that's what's missing now. When people go to narrative films, they think they've gotta go Hollywood & have people acting like someone else & make a completely different story. It's almost like they're afraid to show snippets, like the way you do, of people just being themselves relating to one another. You could have those narrative elements, have them be real, have them work in a large format, have the added element of a narrative coming in & out but still have it be the real thing.

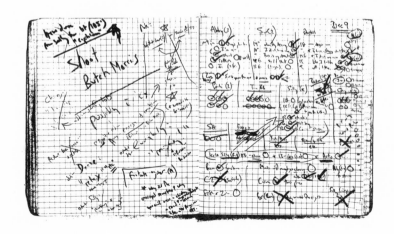

This woman isn't in control ("Oh, boy!") She what she why, um, luckless. I mean, women ("wait-a-minute") women, I mean shit they're gonna get get involved in the strain, splice (hot), & then have you release it.

Meier-Hancock. Do 100 perfect splices in a row before you procede on to original. Scraping is the hardest part. Always use fresh cement. Dip brush in bottle, too much is better than not enough, tap twice on rim to rid of excess, swipe twice to rid of air bubbles. Plug in splicer an hour in advance, then the faster the better: by the time you reclose the bottle, it's time to reopen the splicer. The glue runs whichever direction you apply: top to right, bottom to left (this can be important; when A/B-rolling it should flow onto black leader). A good splice lasts forever, but if you have lots you should go soon to interneg or CRI for preservation.

HH: Narrative's such a loaded word, in the sense of something that's artificially symmetrical, where it has a happy ending or an ending at all, that just seems like bullshit, but if narrative is like a realistic picture of life, then that's interesting maybe to me. I mean, I could never sit down & think up a story, my mind doesn't work that way & I wouldn't be into it. It usually is repulsive to me when somebody else does.

ZORN: I don't think you have to think of a narrative as thinking up a story. A narrative, to me, is just another level of communication, another level of dialog that can exist. Someone in the audience, not the person who initiated what's being looked at, not the artist, justifying a series of unrelated events or images or sounds, weaves it together in their own mind to create a thread & that thread is the narrative. So your films are already dealing with a kind of narrative.

HH: especially MONEY. . .

ZORN: Narrative doesn't automatically mean, "Ok this is my sell-out movie to make it on my next step to Hollywood" or something, which is what everybody else thinks. I don't think it has to be that way. I think narrative elements can be used in a really interesting way & I don't see anybody using them in that way yet.

ABBY: Nobody wants to deal with the complications of reality. Fiction is more simple, usually. It's definitely sustaining one's imagination & life & liveliness, that's the political effort of films is like to manifest life instead of these dopey closed stories that bracket off the world into a fiction that takes you away from anything you can deal with, I'm not even talking about taking you away from anything that you can deal with & change actively but taking you away from what you can appreciate actively. . . Another thing about movies is they're always the same & in some ways that's like reassuring I guess but it also seems like one might look for another way to structure the universe, particularly when access to so many different parts of the world, say living in a city there's like thousands of realities that I can experience on my way from my apartment to the bodega, particularly living in this apartment building, many more than there was living in suburban New Jersey. If you're looking for a corner of the world that nobody looked, nobody paid attention to.

FLESH spoke MERGING. ALBUM spoke FACT.
Liquid to within suction to point to the next plastic wrap that they can describe writing that would work a little. What it means, too.

ALAN: Probably not from the point of view of the person who consumes the art by listening to it or by reading it or whatever, but from the point of view of the person who makes it, I mean the first thing that occurred to me in terms of writing was really how poor the language was as a tool, how totally inadequate it was. It's as if you get up in the morning & someone says this pile of garbage here, this is for you to use today, & I want you to make something beautiful & something that will last for awhile & something that people will like. At first it was in terms of referentiality & stuff, you just don't have the words to express what you want to express, not in any mundane way & certainly not in a romantic way, but just in a simple utilitarian way. By giving it a context you would get a little closer to what you wanted to say, but then the more I look at it, the whole tools, not just the referentiality of the process, but all of the tools involved in the bringing of those referents to life are like really clumsy too. What made me think of this was the really dumb state of video art, how inadequate it is to take care of what we're capable of thinking. They say that the average human uses 5% of their brain. It might be in part, although it's impossible to say which came first, because the *tools* that we have are also in our brains. It's an incredible mechanism because the material is in there & the tools are in there & to a great extent they're not separable. But the tools that we have for using the materials that are in our brain are really not adequate to move more than that percentage of what we're capable of thinking or conceiving. It's almost as if in this one place, which from other points of view is many places or no place, but in this one organism, the human brain, you have both, in that way it's the same as the language, but you have both the materials, which you could say are like the nouns, & you have the tools, which you could say are like the verbs, to make a really kind of childish metaphor. You have the material for what is being expressed & you have the tools for that expression but they're locked together, so there's a kind of identity of them & it makes it difficult. The function of art, I think, is to separate them & get them far enough apart that they can develop & grow & evolve or mutate. But it's as if they're so close that the mechanisms of thought can't get far enough from the materials of thought to change themselves & the materials can't get far enough from the mechanisms to get the rest that they need to generate more materials.

Buying & selling means only more money against thought.

HIT ME!

REVOLUTION (what's possible) lost. I don't think I could take that. Feminist workers organize everybody's situations! Situation has a crisis (93) about their position over MONEY (motherfucker). Would you give me $2? $2.50? $2.7—society, & also MONEY (motherf---). $1300, haha. All my needs are taken care of & that the MONEY will do, yes, MONEY will do. Trying to get you, you filmmakers, immediate dollars, uh, at least 100,000. More MONEY for me. The rich people have 20% MONEY, because He'll be able to have them 'born again.' It's not gonna cost you enough MONEY. Money, everybody, aggh!! Try to, uh, try to still have, Henry, has resulted in severe needless interest, y'know. But they will, in fact, get everyone together like MONEY, which I'm slightly vague about.   "Yeah."

James Sherry

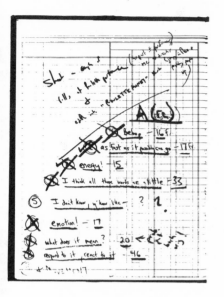

HH: Everybody's effort is kind of partial. Even partial within their limited capabilities.

ALAN: Maybe talent is just the ability to use the whole 5%. But don't you when you're making, when you're producing something like that, when you're editing the film, don't you feel this incredible kind of expansiveness. And you feel like you're pushing your brain to its limit and your eyes and your hands and your person and your self and you're really like extending yourself further out in relation to everything that exists to a greater extent than you could in any other way, really? And yet, then when this feeling subsides & the activity is momentarily over or when your heightened awareness of it is momentarily gone, then you look at it & you say, "Good God!" Not how horrible it is, although you might have that feeling too, but at least what an incredible paucity there is of material & method & so on to express what I just felt was there. I mean you really get this rush of, & I don't think there's anything trippy about it, it's just like the mind finally working at a little more than its potential, but you get this rush of real feeling of potential & size & scope & connection with a lot of things or everything or whatever & then when you look at what you've *got* as a result of that experience, that's what I'm talking about is this difference between what you're able to express & what you've actually experienced.

HH: & when other people look at it & they don't even. . .

ALAN: They don't even get *that*. You work all night for one metaphor & really hammer it into the structure & nobody even sees it.

HH: Yeah, but if you quit doing it, then you don't have the experience either.

ALAN: Yeah, you can, I think.

HH: Well, sometimes I take walks, or just going somewhere, & sometimes I'm really *on* to where it's just like a film, my eyes are jumping all over the place & I'm seeing all kinds of stuff & I'm fitting together the movement & in fact I don't even know in these cases whether I've trained myself to look a certain way by the kinds of films I make or whether the films I make are the way they are because of the way that I *do* look, but yeah & so I might have a moment of real exhilaration just in real life, I mean you *have* to, because your work is always going to be real partial. It's just impossible that your work is going to encompass the whole world. You don't have the whole world. You're just a part of it, anyway, & I mean I guess everybody, people that are not artists, have moments of exhilaration where they really feel like they're comprehending a part of the world & things have meaning for a minute or just are producing an extraordinary amount of pleasure just in & of themselves. But, that's very passive. It's kind of like a rich person's way of going through life, right? You just take everything that the world has to give you without adding something to it.

"Too spaced."

So Alan was drunk. So. "Finished"

Di: "Why what?"
 A: ("Be a fool, y'know")
Di: "Yeah"
Su: "Why ⌇⌇⌇"

ALAN: Often that's why it's so great to travel, just a change of scene & place can be an incitement to that kind of experience. I know that if I get up & go to work on the same bus the chances of my having an experience like that of real enrichment & newness & totality & strength is much less likely than if I get up on Saturday morning & drive out to Pennsylvania & see the sun through the trees for the first time in two months. But it's good to create something as you go along, because a lot of people either don't have that kind of experience, really *don't* I think, or they're not aware of how unique it is & therefore they don't value it as a part of their life. But I think the value of making something as a result of that experience or in the context of it or for no good reason at all is kind of a reminder to people that that kind of experience is possible & the ability to make that kind of reminder & to make it beautiful enough & structurally strong enough etc. that it can sustain itself certainly beyond the period of its making & last at least for a while after that & continue to affect people is reason enough to do it.

Morose moments don't sync up & distribution, as a whole is totally fucked.

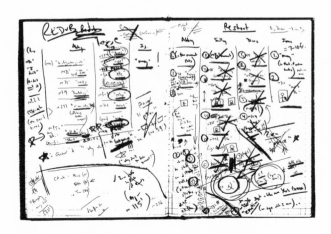

"Torp/hmmm"   Well, yeah, it does.

HH: Well, also, if you just go in pursuit of pleasure like this, say if you define this experience as pleasure, & you lead a hedonistic existence to maximalize this kind of experience, after a while you end up falling back into your own neuroses. Nothing is sharp enough to affect you after a while. You have your own kind of little circles that you spin around in & waste time. I mean I can be happy for a long period of time just passively enjoying the world, travelling or just walking around New York or going to a lot of art events, if ever there's a period it's possible to see a lot of good art events in a row again, maybe this can continue for a while if you're lucky & there's a lot of stimulation & you just keep going on it, but then when it comes to an end you hit even more of a void. It becomes like a drug. Whereas making something, you can work on something when you're in this kind of really void period & pull yourself—well that's another psychological reason, maybe equally as selfish. But in fact you do make something that's beyond just your own personal needs.

ALAN: Even if it's not, at least you're claiming responsibility for making the world for yourself, for that moment even. Instead of, like you were saying, getting into whatever kind of head trip is most convenient for you, or for one as an individual, to be in in order to happen upon those experiences, like go back to nature or take heroin. I mean those guys, a heroin addict certainly has an incredible experience in a certain way. I mean, y'know, I've never been an addict. I can't speak about anything more than the experience of it occasionally. But you can see that they have in a certain sense a very rich experience on certain levels, but they're not open to other levels & they're certainly not making it for themselves buying it. I mean it's all very confused. That's why it's so much fun to keep talking about it & keep going around & around & around, right? And the confusing thing you realize in a certain way you're just chasing your own tail & then you're chasing a tail that you made & then you're talking about chasing a tail that was alive in the world for an instant one morning when the sun shone.

Alright, move & talk!

Pooh Kaye

Sally Silvers

Yoshiko Chuma

This is my street & I have a theory about this. This place stinks. Like I I-like, "Capitalism isn't dramatic."

Abby Child

PH

15	well
19	(resync to Croq.)*
28	thoroughly marginalized
48	cured. A future exist-ence in outer space

POOH (2)

+() (SU: "those bad boys are saying mean things about me.")

SALLY (re)

12	("Hit Me" dance)
13	idea (Raf, dark)
15	classes (Raf)
19	(light laugh)
32	(my laugh, then hers)

ZORN (7th)

6	& so

POOH (PIX) (4)

YOSH (PIX) (3)

(& Yosh & Moss... & () scream)

COLOM

(yoddle) (3) the cars*

ARTO () (can be cutup)

MOSS () (close-up ω moneybags)

ABBY (CAN)

12	to strain (movement!)

AL (OR)

12	against

DI (OR)

9	open

JAS

7	home
14	traffic

JAMES: . . . data-based concepts or expert systems or that your work has a certain quality of information that is modular in the same sense that data in a computer is stored. It's also kind of similar to the kind of thing that Ron Silliman does with the New Sentence, where often the content of each sentence, or, in your case, the content of each set of frames, is less important than its relation to the other sets of frames & what you're doing now is almost a visceral, intuitive jux-taposing of those scenes, whereas what you are approaching is the kind of mate-rial that would be very susceptible to analysis of those scenes as pure informa-tional categories without any content. Each one having a specific length, a specific content, a specific character in it, a certain exposure, a certain time of day when it was shot, & all the different variables that you have available to you at any one time. You're playing with these in an intuitive manner; you could carry it further & play with it in a non-intuitive manner. Nobody's yet come up with, but I think they will, principles of organization that are meaningful, not only externally but also internally. That impart meaning to the viewer while one is watching the film, not narrative, not simply slow takes on nature or simply rapid cuts that provoke some kind of emotional response in the viewer that's manipulated by the film-maker, but further meaning because all these kinds of variables that one can work with ought to be able to generate meaning in all kinds of different ways & that meaning doesn't have to be random & it doesn't have to be intuitional. Old art is narrative, descriptive, & intuitional, & that we have to be willing to get away from intuition & from inspiration as much as we're willing to get away from narrative & description, because of the whole notion of the artist as magician is part of what's holding us back. Mystic modernism!

HH: I don't agree with you at all . . .

"The *Man* is across the street. We can't mess with *the Man*."

John Zorn

. . ."& a youth gang is also approaching with baseball bats"

Susie Timmons

in a cemetery

"No, not in a cemetary"

". . .can never remember his name." "Watten (pause), y'know."

"oh" (blush)

It's all available. They try to get you to feel yellow. Oooo (crumbles).

JAMES: You're on the romantic & conservative side of the node of progress because of your excessive reliance on the emotional & intuitional moves or tropes, in the same way that I objected to your talking about Capitalism when you're talking about money as if Capitalism invented money. Another kind of focus that I think exposes your point of view rather than opening the viewer's mind up. Now granted the thing that I've been talking about in terms of using information theory to organize work is also a way of limiting, because it's only by limitation that you can get any accumulation of energy into a piece. I'm not saying that work should be so open-ended that everything diffuses out of it. I think that's a big weakness of a lot of experimental work today.

HH: Well with film there's so many limitations built in, I think that that gives film part of the dynamic that video doesn't have.

JAMES: Another place where there's more work to be done is in the area of *connections*. In computer language, every part of speech is of equal importance. In English, in most of our social contacts, there are certain things that are given a high priority—nouns & verbs. Articles & prepositions & conjunctions, you can take them or leave them most of the time. But in information theory the accuracy of every single part of speech is, one is required to be equally accurate. If you have a wrong conjunction the info cannot be processed. Likewise in your films you have the potential for working closely with parts of film language that are not sufficiently attended to by other filmmakers. There's so many openings & that's why your film is so powerful for me, because it's formative, really groundbreaking in the sense that it opens up huge areas for analysis & thought. It's not so much exploring all of them, but it keeps opening them up, for me, & that's the sense that you're on the progressive edge of the node.

HH: I mean I could see making a work in real time & having certain interlocking programs that the computer was editing & then the viewer or the maker would be overriding certain decisions & making certain decisions spontaneously & be composing in real time with channels of real time info coming in, composing on live TV.

JAMES: Sounds very expensive.

HH: Well it's not possible at all right now, but there's no reason why it shouldn't be at some point.

"I know Henry always could last"   "Relax!"

Men tell you women envy cock. I think it's really shitty (good, good)...but just coming, like maybe next to the toned possibility & factories in Outer Space*, I think all those words are a little rotten, when they decay. I can't remember. I, I think it's clearly, well, research when to press the button (Thank you, America) It's only a symbol to lead the Soviets in a little emotion. I appreciate it. You want a little? These are off. . .

```
         POOH (2)

         PH

 6"      I like these places,
         they're gonna
10"      ---alright---
16fr     fucker, they're gonna
 9       threatened
10       well
 9       artist(s)
 6"      I can't hear a thing

         CARMEN

 9fr     films

         BR (CAN)

 5"      beneath me (beep)

         ABBY (CAN)

 4"      to strain

         COLOM

         (yoddle) (1)

         POOH (pix) (3)

         YOSH (pix) (5)

         ZORN

 6       or so
```

JAMES: What I think is that right now people are using art & all this computer stuff in some sense in a computer-centered way, or in an information-centered way, & I think that the reason we're making thinking machines is not to make a machine that thinks like a person or to teach people to think more like machines, but rather to use this process to illuminate the way in which people think. And that's where I see the strongest opening in your work. It seems to me that the more that we can do to learn about the way in which we think or the way in which we act by illuminating or highlighting aspects of more limited modes of thought, such as computer thought or computer organization of information, to clarify the way in which we think the better off we are & it seems to me that that is most readily done by applying limited modes of thought such as computer language structures or computer syntax to film studies. Instead of applying hardware to content, apply software to content. What's interesting about your work is the thought-concepts, not the mechanical concepts. What you're doing is synthesizing new material; you're not simply deconstructing things anymore. You've gotten down to the point of a single frame & you can't get any smaller.

*Studies have been done.

My pen &, uh, your papers. . .remember?

"We don't have time to read."   oh?

(snd.)

Feb 4:	12 min 33 sec
Feb 6:	452 ft 21 fr
Thurs:	453.17 (12.35)
Fri:	456.25 (12.41)
Weds:	458'19
	459'22 (12'45)

Feb 14, 1984

A3

8"	motion pictures
8fr	agree
9	y'know

RON

12	oneself
10	some
9	(laugh)
7	but our

PH

18"	it wd be easy to break strikes in outer space
10"	---alright---
6"	I like these places, they're gonna
6"	I can't hear a thing
9fr	artists
9	threatened

HH: So you actually think of your writing as similar to filmmaking?

BRUCE: Yeah, cause I'm going out & shooting. It's all on these little note-cards. It's not visually oriented. It's more like the process of shooting & editing seems similar. I.e., I don't sit down at my desk & write a poem anymore. I'll sit down at my desk with hundreds of notecards & I'll just lay them out on the page & I'll see if I can string a few of them together in an exciting way & then I'll have a little phrase, etc.

HH: So your writing is heavily involved in editing then?

BRUCE: Absolutely.

HH: Cause some of your peers absolutely don't believe in editing.

BRUCE: Absolutely, they do not. So it's just like a different way & I think it's related to this thing about thematic focus.

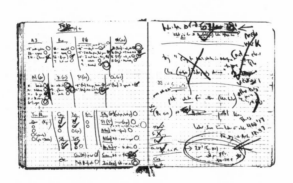

PH (snd)

21	(Pooh): and, uh (2)
16	(Sally): & I think that
16	(ST): and, uh (1)
13	(Sally): Absolutely

AL (OR)

15	breasts
14	substance
11	to go
11	to mean
6	(laugh)

DI (OR)

10	& that
9	y'know
8	work

ST (snd)

8"	(Pooh): Thank you, America
6"	(Chas): which isn't too clear

CHAS (SND)

5"	(Pooh): I appreciate it

JAMES: . . . A very highly-charged film. Extremely angry. A sense of social injustice pervades the movie. By the intense sarcasm & cynicism of the content of the different sections—having the dancer juxtaposed to the airplane . . . just having money as the central theme without even showing any of the benefits that money as a system of exchange provides to all of us on an everyday basis. So it's like focussing on the horrors of this medium of exchange, both structural & particular, in the sense of the warplane. So I think it's a very out-raged political statement, almost muckraking in a certain sense, which is what allies you to this group of artists, I think, most closely.

HH: Right, cause I thought of it more as being, in that sense, a portrait of what they talk about all the time. And money, I mean, it had no title when I started it. It just kept coming up & up & up & then I began to dwell on it as I saw that it had a lot of interesting possibilities.

Too long on that system's, uh, system:

Tactics vs. strategy, perfection vs. progress

```
           TOM BB
(3)+(1)(pix only)+(1)(pix=Skel.
Crew)
           CROQ (3)
           SH (2)
           YOSH (2+1pix)
           T&F (3)
           POOH (2)
           SALLY
10"        (my laugh, her laugh)
           ST
9"         (laugh)
16fr       (laugh; for laugh sect.)
           A (LES)
10fr       (pause)
           AL (1ST)
21fr       more in anger
           ABBY (CAN)
4"         to strain
           CARMEN
10fr       film
           ZORN (7TH ST)
6fr        or so
```

SUSIE: . . . to say that by taking into consideration the audience's existence & that they have a certain attention span & beyond that point they're not going to hear what you're doing anymore & they're going to start feeling *bad*, y'know . . . I don't want to endure, I want to be entertained. I don't want to *endure* somebody's art work. Then it becomes like a social obligation.

HH: Well it affects the quality of the attention, too.

SUSIE: I'm finding that being boring is the worst thing.

HH: & like boring poetry readings are the worst of all.

SUSIE: You can't get up.

HH: It feels like church.

SUSIE: It's exactly the same thing, it's like school.

HH: & I keep thinking, "What am I doing this of my own free will?"

HIT ME!

Peace lies, not without problems, now in the working class (I guess.)
Why isn't it functioning?

ZORN: I don't think we're going to get to a period where there's no avant-garde experimental film being made. I think it's being made, it just looks different.

HH: Maybe it's being made. It's just not being shown.

ZORN: Someone's out there making it. There's always something going on. Because the Anthology went through an identity crisis & refused to change, it disappeared. I mean they wouldn't accept *any* new films into their precious "100 films of perfection" from the mid-60's or whatever. They were killing themselves & they didn't even know it. They were killing the whole movement & they didn't even know it by refusing new filmmakers into their treasure trove. I mean that's really sad. How closed-minded can you be, for someone that's supposed to be so open. I mean they disappeared & you're still around. There's gotta be someone out there doing it. I think we're not aware because it looks so *different*.

HH: What does it look like?

ZORN: I don't know. How can we know? A lot of times I go to things & I think, "Well I never saw anything like this before & I think it's total shit. But wait a minute, maybe this is great."

HH: But what happens to me is I go to things & I think, "I've seen this so many times."

ZORN: Well, see, people used to say that about my shit. People used to say that all the time, "Oh it's the same bullshit you've heard. An all-night jam session with special instrumental effects. Just a lot of noises." That's what I used to hear all the time. And now it's like, "totally original." I'm doing the same fucking stuff.

HH: Yeah, well, as your work develops it becomes clearer, anybody's work, becomes clearer what you're doing.

ZORN: But that's why you have to doubt your first impressions when you see something & you say, "I've seen this a million times before." Sometimes you have to give it the benefit of the doubt.

HH: I mean when I'm in an open-minded mood, which I am now . . . I mean when I'm really involved in my work it either has to be something that's gonna give me some ideas or something that's gonna relax me or I've got no use for it, at that time, well that's not totally true. It depends on how generous I feel. I mean, usually when we talk about that kind of impression, it's usually a younger artist, right?

"What does it mean?" That's the thing, to mean. Five or ten years from now. . . "DAYS, hahah"

ZORN: Always.

HH: & they're not fully developed.

ZORN: & there are silly elements.

HH: & they have to work through all that same crap & it's a matter of looking & seeing if there's something there. Well, that's where it helps to see people's work again a year or so later & you see . . .

ZORN: Where they've gone.

. . .was all trigger muscles drawn (punk), who knows? Stroke! anyhow. . .

```
         CARMEN

         all the time
         filmmakers
Apr 6:   470.01=13.03
Apr 8:   468.04=13.00
Apr 12:  471:27 or 13'06"
Apr 15:  472.17=13.07
Mon:     472.26 (13'07")
May 2:   473'10 (or 13.08)


May 3, 1984

         CARMEN
22       try to, uh, try to
15       uh, it, I
 6       something
snd only--born again

         CHAS
10       (laughter)
replacement scenes (KK 10-77)
(also--we'll give you a copy &
       go to Russia)

         BR (CAN)
10"      all our needs are taken
         care of
Carmen--all the time
(Su--out)
```

HH: There is an awkward, funky aspect to people's work in the first few years, maybe the first 5 years that they're doing it, depending on how late in their life they start it & how much of a vengeance they start with. There's kind of an awkward aspect to anything anybody in their 20's does.

ZORN: People thrive on that shit.

HH: There's also a kind of dead element to anything that anybody over 30 does. That's just so great. You get ignored, or people are just embarrassed by you, for all these years & then suddenly you're an old fart. There might be like a week or two when you're there. Then you're an old fart doing the same old shit. I get sick of hearing all that Zorn shit over & over—when is something *new* gonna come along?

ZORN: Yeah, man, then you try to do something different & it's "copping out."

Because I hear it in sight, you just want me to call Griffith, or an indian, don't you?
"Absolutely"

Griffith's mother & my mother were both surnamed Oglesby.

Someone presses her butt in his nip (pft) but our feet said, "Zorn, ah ah, normal / turned to 45."

Everything else hatched out of my brain, repeat, in / over / & up, uh, this & that lip-trade as they were fun & money

". . .is, um, vague, it's very vague, it's not, it's nothing in particular."

Hit me

Diane Ward

Charles Bernstein

He's doing everything except quakes ("away from home" HOME!) *and* T-shirts ("Move to Russia") *and* communicating emotionally one to another ("tonight?")

and one can feel free to express one's emotions   (scream)

CHARLES: What happens is, after I was shot everything blanked out for a couple of minutes & I don't remember anything for what seemed to be some indefinite period of time. Then I felt very, very relaxed. I felt like I was in a park, but it was very pleasant, kind of like Southern California, blue sky & maybe about 75 degrees, very clear, & I felt I was lying not on the ground but a few inches above the ground & that I was going up just slightly, very slightly, up to the level of 4 or 5 feet & I felt a sense of warmth, of contentment, & the events of my life didn't pass by actually, but certain highlights, certain of the more positive things kind of were in a list that I saw, in writing actually, but in a language that I hadn't previously known but was able to understand, kind of red letter dates & so on that I saw kind of not so much in the sky but against the horizon, & then that sort of faded away & the sky became suffused with a kind of orangy, kind of like Orange Julius because it had that foamy, y'know, that kind of foamy as if there was some egg mixed in, & that began to kind of close in on me & then I began to feel this kind of orangy foamy stuff kind of come all around. . . It was a very pleasant sensation of being kind of enveloped in this orange kind of thick foamy stuff & I remember laughing & giggling & then I blacked out again.

HH: Then what happened?

CHARLES: Oh, then I realized it was just a toy gun.

Anyway, Capitalism: it's not so well!

Election lost to vicious bureaucrat (he's a businessman) (p'duke puddee k'dee) that would then create division & radical elements.

Respond to it, react to it!   (scream)

Yoshiko Chuma

```
          ABBY (CAN)
10fr     blank
15       put...PUT
(replacement pix w track floating
close-up)

          A(LES)--pause

          SU

          out, because he'll be
          able to
          pause (I just haven't
          paid
          of/of/of
          I would (pause)
          clearly
(2 trial replacements for
"I guess")

          COLOM (yoddle) (1)

          YOSH

(new pix (bondage) w scream, but
overlap scream & "hit me" here for
mix)

          SALLY

(my laugh & hers)

          AL (OR)

          "/belie"

          DI (OR)

1'        (pause) it's this--
          y'know
          work

          PH

          to, uh

          SALLY (dance dub) (7)

          PIX SLUGS
             Zorn
             Susie
             Abby

          YOSH (DANCE)

          ARTO

             etc.

May 4:    477.23=13'15"
May 7:    477.28=13'16"
May 8:    479.04=13'18"
June 19 (Tues): 492.32 (13'41")
June 22:  494.29 (13'44)
June 25:  495.35 (13'46)
     26:  498'39 (or 13min51sec)
```

ABBY: I think money is censorship. We've talked about all this before.

HH: Not on this tape.

ABBY: Ok, like I was actually surprised to read in your proposal *your* concern with the representational image, because I always thought you actually, I don't know, it was a fairly, you know it was THE argument for representational imagery, like an interest in what carries meaning or what seems to *have* a lot of meaning. You didn't seem to really be discussing what kinds of meaning, but anyway so what interested me was what you thought about that.

HH: What do you mean you were surprised?

ABBY: Well I've just never heard you discuss it as an issue.

HH: Didn't you ever think my movies were always very concerned with representation?

ABBY: No, I thought in some ways the formal ones, I mean I know that they were things you *loved* which then allowed you to play formal manipulations with them, but in fact no.

HH: Well it was a different era for one thing, I think. And also those were like learning how to, I mean I knew that I had to do this kind of experimentation to learn how to make films like I wanted to make films. Yeah, right, the rhythms are more important for a long time than the, uh, but that was when I was living in San Francisco & that was a more meditative environment. I'm trying to make more aggressive, out-in-the-world things now. It's not a very meditative period, but also I think it's important. If you want to change the world, you finally at some point gotta start trying to do it. I don't mean aggressive as far as being manipulative, more like Rock n Roll is aggressive, like you're blowing up & this is something that blows you up too but in a good way. It's not quite that simple. All the drives & urges that are going on behind my films are not so simple as the adolescent drives behind rock, but there's some of that I think. I mean I don't think Ernie could ever make films like these or me like him because it's a different kind of craziness, y'know.

"If you're not getting enough here in America, go to Russia!"

NO!   hahahaa

Abby Child

words on snd-pulls-track:

(13-C2-research)
20-Ron-much more rapidly
17-Ron-which included a-
15-Ron-they had a
 9-Ron-problem
29-Ron-uh, at least 100,000
13-Al-eyes
23-Ron-has resulted in severe
17-Al-noises
12-Ron-in order to-
11-Al-torment
 6-Ron-do
11-Al-locked(honk)
22-Sally-boring, tedious
22-C2-on the other hand
 7-Colom-Henry
13-C2-eye(oy)
 8-Sally-well
10-Sally-well
26-Carmen-if you don't talk fast
(re to Yosh/Z/Carm)

A4(RE)

difficult
y'know
up, uch is to say--
y'know, 8/--
& I find this very

ZORN (TV) ()
TOM (BB) ()
FRITH & Z ()
MOSS (re-Roul) ()
CROQ (re) (3)
T&F (re) (3)
ARTO (2 track moan) ()

ABBY (movement) (re) ()
POOH   "   "   "   ()
SALLY   "   "   "   ()
(YOSH   "   "   "   (3))

ABBY (4-pix only) (4)

AL(Or): "M" (2)
DI(Or): "M" (2)

snd--misc "/" (7)
        extra scream
        etc

ABBY: Well what do you think of the choice of that—

HH: It's not a choice so much. Well it's a choice in a sense, a choice not to make dopey shit like everybody else does, the choice though is to make films that are appropriate to *my* consciousness or sensibility. Beyond that it's not a choice of what my consciousness or my sensibility is. I mean I guess it's a lot of choices over my whole life. How much control does one have over one's formation? Where does personality begin? It's not like completely thrust upon somebody. I don't know how much is volitional, though, or how much is accidental or whatever.

ABBY: Personality emerges in the decision to not have any personality in the work. But then also there's the personality in the rhythm, which is what leads you to make a *hot* film rather than a more meditatively-paced film. Your silent films had a meditative sense which the sound definitely is not. If you showed your recent films silently I think they would be more meditative too. They would fall into an image patterning. It's the sound that's the real disrupt. Yeah, from PLA-GIARISM on you could argue that your films are more involved with the representational image, but in some ways I don't feel that's true. I feel like you've substituted people for architecture & in a very cubistic way & what's *interesting* is I'm not sure that the image is carrying more meaning, but you are having words be full of meaning, but I'm not sure you're approaching the representational image.

That's for those down here in, uh, Belize, but our careless purpose, a part of which moving is never kilter. Hmmph, what is that to do with *that*   STOP!

You like that?

```
DI(Or) 14fr--to stay
AL(Or) 11-needless
       11-shot

SU** -I would
     -I just haven't

ZORN(board): "improvise"

pix(29fr @):
     Sally in front of
       plane
     Abby finger to head

Ron-5
Di-6
Carmen-7
      13

C2--so
C(LES)-12-program
```

```
Weds 27:    499.36 (13-53)
Thurs 28:   500.29 (13-54)
Fri 29:     500.24
Mon         498.28
later       499.15
Tues, July 3:  500.11 (13'53)
July 16:    502.16
July 17:    502.30 (13'57)
final       515.17 (14'19)
```

```
PREMIERE:  November 2, 1984
           Collective for Living Cinema
```

```
PERFORMANCE:  November 30, 1984
              Roulette
              228 W. Broadway, NYC
```

Speakers:

Bruce Andrews
Abigail Child
Alan Davies
Susie Timmons
Diane Ward
        &
James Sherry as "Mr. Money"

Movers:

Pooh Kaye
Sally Silvers

Musicians:

John Zorn (alto, reeds, duckcalls
           water & vocals)
Jim Staley (trombone & drainpipe)
Charles Noyes (percussion)
Butch Morris (cornet)
Ikue Mori (percussion)
Christian Marclay (turntables)
Tom Cora (cello)
Ciro Baptiste (Brazilian percussion)

Audio:

David Weinstein (controls)
Jim Biederman (tapes)
```

**HH:**  Oh I feel less with PLAGIARISM, more with RADIO ADIOS, & much more with MONEY & the thing you were commenting on is that I want to do it that much more &, in a way, if I want to expand out to a larger work, that's the area to expand.

**ABBY:**  It's the traditional area to expand, the conventional one. Just what you're saying in a way about marginality is like you're going to use a certain thing that's out in the world & transform it.

**HH:**  Right, I mean I never thought that I might not ever approach more conventional filmmaking, but I wanted to approach it from a totally backwards way. I remember years ago that I wanted to make a movie that people might think was almost like a normal movie, but that would really be like totally weird, I mean completely, absolutely, anybody that was sophisticated to whatever degree that they were sophisticated about film could see how weird it was & all these other things going on, but there would be this veneer on the top. Uh, but I mean I don't want to be *that* conventional.

**ABBY:**  It seems to me that you've talked about how you're making it more interesting & more detail & it is more colorful & there is more movement, but except for the obvious metaphors, like dancing in garbage or standing in front of ruin, the real heavy-duty-city-straightforward background, the street stuff just seems like 'out on the street,' it's more like the cubistic issue, it's texture/color/movement, it's not *really* the meaning, which is fine. It could be that the sound *is*; you're investigating an aspect of the detailing of the frame.

**HH:**  You read a novel & that's like saying that all the scenes are not what has meaning, what has meaning are the way the words are put together & maybe the development of the character or something.

**ABBY:**  Fine, & the way you put your words together seems to be carrying the meaning, but the way you put your images together. . . Well I'm just wondering is the representational image . . . ok, like if you look at a Bosch painting, well it's a representative image of a fantasy life, but if you're talking about in a way out of abstraction towards a frame that could be as complex, I mean in some Utopia, as a Hieronymus Bosch painting, y'know, filled with figures & little events & scenes, kind of what Tati is looking for in PLAYTIME in 90mm where things are happening in the corners of the frames, so if that it's one thing, although I think you almost fight against it by putting a figure in the center. It's almost as if there was a Bosch that had a portrait on top of it & it was like the background was tapestry. Maybe the representative is in fact the portrait of the people.
```

Girls kicking their legs.

Can't pass her, Pete? Que pasa, people?

HIT ME!

HH: Although it's not exactly a portrait because different people come across different on film. There's people who come across much stronger on film than in real life & other people who come across much weaker, or just barely come across. In a lot just to keep some people from coming across so dead I just had to get them jazzed out of their minds so they come across as totally frantic crazies, which in a way I wanted that & certainly encouraged that franticness. It was just like the whole process was so frantic that it was hard not to have the acting be frantic too.

ABBY: Well that's another question, which is what does acting have to do with movies. Actually what it has to do is that acting is the history of movies, it doesn't have anything intrinsic to do with movies whatsoever. It's interesting what an odd origin.

HH: I guess, although you think about it & Vertov's article is one thing, but on the other hand it can't be like this huge accident that 99% of movies are acted.

ABBY: Oh no, I think that's about the mirror. We like looking at human bodies, because drama's gone nowhere.

HH: You're saying that *words* are what I'm concerned about with meaning, but on the other hand most of the time people when they see the film can't understand the words or can't hear the words, which is one reason I'm doing this book because here are all the words. If you know what they are you can always hear them. I always hear all of them. But most of the time it's shown with different systems I can't imagine how anyone can hear half of them & it always puzzles me. I can't tell what people are hearing & what they're not, & so whatever that might have been my intention, it's not what's carrying the meaning.

(joker)

F'doo, (pre-) make-up mirrrr. Poe last tension. (background noise, pause, then toot)

Flashback = memory, flash forward = prophecy

Need it again?   We'll give you a copy.

ABBY: But I wonder, for a viewing where they don't understand the words it seems to me that the meaning is much closer to NORTH BEACH. The film doesn't seem to be about money whatsoever except in the word comment upon it. What does it have to do with money? I mean that became the unity that you chose because it's a deluxe attention-getter & also a state of mind we're living in & increased & you can extend it real easy, but I don't think the film, I mean the words talk about money in interesting ways, but I feel like in a way that the image aspect is a color/movement field, which is fine.

HH: Film is just one big accident. The fact that it works, that a procession of pictures creates motion. And the way sync is matched. There's no reason for the format; it was just some guy working for Edison. The only reason for the video format is that RCA was able to make vacuum tubes in this certain format in the 1940s. Even the projection speed, it's already changed at least once, at one time it was variable, the projectionist was a participant, now the guy who did the effects for 2001 & BLADERUNNER says it should be 60 fps.

ABBY: A lot of people approach film because they like the physicality of it.

HH: Do you? I don't love sitting down at the rewinds & rolling film back & forth. I like looking at it & a lot of my ideas come from examining the strip, but I hate working at the rewinds actually. I love working on the flatbed. It's more like instant gratification. There's so many delays in filmmaking; it's not like painting where you can be working all the time. There's money & the weather & getting people together. I sort of appreciate the delay getting rushes back from the lab; it gives you some distance. Also the fact of the cost limiting how much you can shoot I think is an advantage over video where you can shoot all you want & how can you possibly deal with all that material? I think that also makes the image more dominant in film than the sound. I think it's not just the smallness of the image that makes the sound more dominant in video, as you see with something like stereo MTV. You can easily record all the sound you might ever want. It's pervasive, like Peter was saying about television. You depend very heavily on having background music in your life. It's not that you can't stand silence. You don't have silence. It's not even the street noises you want to drown out; it's like all the motors & stuff in your place, the refrigerator motor, the heating system, the plumbing, I've even been in situations where the sound of my electric clock was driving me crazy. I don't know what that says about your consciousness. . . It's hard to sit down to classical music & listen for the kind of development that the composer intended. You can certainly sit down in front of a live group playing this music & follow it in that way. I find sometimes I can do it lying in bed at night with the lights off, but I think a lot of the music we listen to, especially in New York, is aimed towards shorter, more fragmented . . . Cage, Kagel,

This material & interview text entered
into the Segue IBM-PC by Sharon Gary.

Zorn . . . any order is ok. That's another physical restriction of film, the pieces are not mobile where you can switch them around, which may be the case in some future laser system. When that comes we can all quit making experimental films & write programs for people to use to get interesting viewings out of their vast videodisc libraries.

ZORN: Well, what else can we say about your new film?

HH: That sounds like the kind of question I might ask.

POOH: Do you know that Kathy Acker is my cousin?

"Something there in the trained rectangle. Surfaces *imply* sensuality, that is, there's variety of texture, and yet, technology's brilliant illusion finally nothing for the body to grasp. Angles advance downward to establish a rhythmic separation. Mottled messages are sent on a common plane from alternating points and stop abruptly at the wall, which is the eye."
—Diane Ward, "Independent Screws"

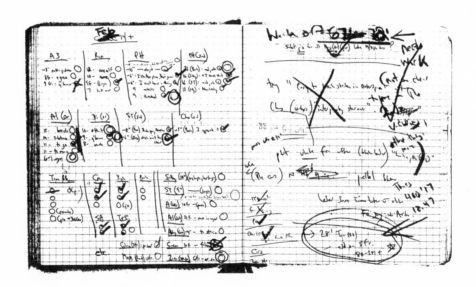

On the other hand, the music forest with us in any odds
"W,"
"W,"
"W"
like bobbing material, so--------

REVENGE!

The Performance

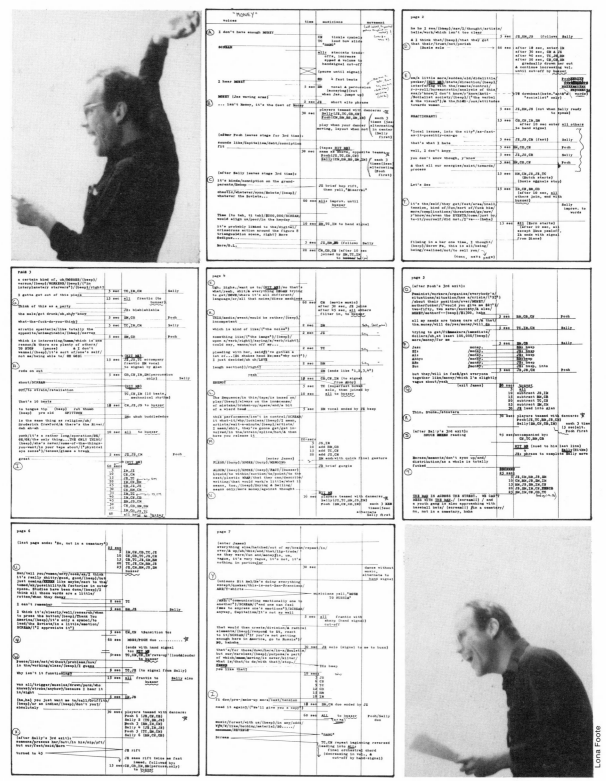

Henry Hills directing

Lona Foote

ACKNOWLEDGEMENTS

I wish to thank most of all those artists who appeared in my film (see last page) & particularly those who additionally contributed words to the text of this book. I also want especially to thank those who contributed money to the Segue Money Fund: Frances O. & Henry L. Hills, Richard A. Oglesby, Margaret H. Fairleigh, Dr. Joel D. Epstein, Bruce & Mary Anna Edenfield, William F. Rector, Fielder Cook, M. Lamar Oglesby, Rick & Barbara Painter, Marie Brown, Clint Palmer, John F. Oglesby, & Stuart L. Oglesby. MONEY was begun with a grant from the National Endowment for the Arts (#21-3411-191, 1982). It was completed & the performance & much of this book done through a grant from the New York State Council on the Arts. As the NEA funds ran out & before the Segue Money drive, I supported the project as a laborer for Lower Manhattan Construction Company & as a carpenter's assistant to Charlie DiJulio. Much of the footage was shot on an old CBS News camera, a Frezzolini single-system rig rented cheap from Rafik, from whom I purchased all of the Ektachrome reversal stock on which the film was shot. I have edited my sound films primarily at Young Filmmakers (now Film/Video Arts): PLAGIARISM & KINO DA! in Times Square & RADIO ADIOS & MONEY at Pennebaker's on West 86th Street. I am deeply indebted to Bastian & Marlies Cleve for loaning me their house in Los Angeles for the month of January 1983, during which time I solved the structure of the piece after many months of tortured floundering, & to David & Diana Wilson who helped keep me sane during this month. Thanks also to Peter Seaton & Mr. E who shared viewings on the flatbed of the developing stages in the making of this & my previous films & to Steve Ledbetter whose good sense amplified many ideas. All of my lab work was done at Cinelab (now Le-Jen Labs). Thanks Marvin, Benito, Fred, Betty. My transfers & final mix were done at Magno-Sound. Thanks to Maria Pon for the discounts & Aaron Nathanson for the mix. The titles were shot at Animus by Dan Esterman. Abigail Child & I have shared ideas & listened to each other's problems almost daily for the past nine years. Without her loving influence & astute critique this project & much more would never have been. Diane Ward advised & encouraged me at every stage in the making of this book & made it a more pleasant experience. Additional production thanks: James Sherry, Susan Bee, & Freda Mekul. Thousands of pages were xeroxed at Heuston Copy on Waverly near Washington Square. The interview text & the "Moneybin" section were patiently deciphered from the mess I gave her & entered into Wordstar on the Segue IBM-PC by Sharon Gary. All type was set by Accent Graphics, Lincoln, Nebraska. Thanks Michael Jensen. Photographic work by Ken Pelka & St. Marks Graphics. Special thanks to Jon Rubin whose Ludlow Street studio I shared during the first mock-up of this book & on whose J-K optical printer & Pentax I shot the still blow-ups. Back cover photo by Lona Foote. I did the paste-up & mechanicals.

Printed in Ann Arbor, Michigan by McNaughton & Gunn.

Of this first edition 26 copies are lettered A - Z & signed by the author.

Now that you've read the book, SEE THE MOVIE!

MONEY

starring

JOHN ZORN	DIANE WARD	CARMEN VIGIL
SUSIE TIMMONS	SALLY SILVERS	RON SILLIMAN
JAMES SHERRY	DAVID MOSS	MARK MILLER
ARTO LINDSAY	POOH KAYE	PETER HALL
FRED FRITH	ALAN DAVIES	TOM CORA
JACK COLLOM	YOSHIKO CHUMA	ABIGAIL CHILD
CHARLES BERNSTEIN		BRUCE ANDREWS

with

jim staley	ned rothenberg	bob ostertag	charles noyes
butch morris	ikue mori	george lewis	joelle leandre
bill laswell	mark kramer	wayne horwitz	carol emmanuel
robert dick	eugene chadbourne	george cartwright	polly bradfield
coby batty	derek bailey	ciro baptiste	anonymous

TELL YOUR LOCAL PROGRAMMER TO SHOW IT!!

AVAILABLE FOR RENTAL FROM:

Film-Makers' Cooperative
175 Lexington Avenue
New York, New York 10016
(212) 889-3820

and

Canyon Cinema Cooperative
2325 Third Street, Suite 338
San Francisco, California 94107
(415) 626-2255

OTHER FILMS BY HENRY HILLS ALSO AVAILABLE:

PORTER SPRINGS   3
NORTH BEACH
NORTH BEACH   2
PLAGIARISM
KINO DA!
RADIO ADIOS

write for catalogs & current rates